Year 2 Contents

vol ca no

To the student

Everyone loves to write. We write lists to remember things. We write notes and emails to our friends. We write stories and poems, reports and recounts.

When we write, we use **words**. We need to know how to spell the words, so that our reader knows what we are writing about. All our words are made up of **letters**.

In the English alphabet, there are 26 letters—**21 consonants** and **5 vowels**.

a	b	c	d	e	f	g	h	i	j	k	l	m
n	o	p	q	r	s	t	u	v	w	x	y	z

Each letter has a **name** and each letter represents a spoken **sound**. Most **consonants** only have one 'sound'. The **vowels** have a number of different 'sounds'.

Spelling is closely linked to **grammar** (the way we put our sentences together). In this book, you will learn how words look and sound. You will also learn how and when to add endings to words, so that what you write sounds right and makes sense. You will learn any spelling rules that apply. The Top 3 rules are on the back page.

Common endings: -s, -es, -ing, -ed, -y, -er, -est and -ly.

About the author

Del has enjoyed a long career in education as a specialist teacher (Learning Difficulties), education adviser and regional coordinator (English). She has written extensively for parents, teachers and students and is a well-known and respected author nationally and internationally. Her publications cover a diverse range of print and electronic materials in English grammar, spelling, reading, writing and comprehension. She is the author of the popular *Reading Quest* books, a series of readers written for the older, reluctant reader.

Among her latest works are *Blake's Guide to Comprehension*, *Blake's Grammar and Punctuation Guide for lower primary students* and *Targeting Grammar*.

How to Use This Book

Your *Targeting Spelling Activity Book* is set out in units.
Each unit contains two word lists.

SEE & SAY

cat	can
hat	man
sat	ran

SEE & SAY

The words in this list target a particular spelling skill. Look at these words and say them aloud several times. Say the last sound in each word loudly. This will help you to remember what the whole word looks like, and what it sounds like. The *See and Say* words provide a warm-up for the activities that follow.

I
am
the

LOOK & LEARN

These words are used all the time in writing to hold ideas together. They often never change their spelling, no matter where you place them in a text. Learn these words with your eyes, like this:

1. Write the word in large letters on a piece of paper or a whiteboard.
2. Look at the word and say it three times.
3. Close your eyes and picture the word.
4. Open your eyes and check. Is the word the same as your picture?
5. Close your eyes and picture the word again. **Write it in the air with your finger.**
6. Check. Is that the word you wrote?
7. Now, cover the word and write it again from your memory.
8. Check. If the word is not correct, go back to Step 2 and try again.

MEMORY TRAINING Spelling is a skill that requires you to remember the words you want to write. Throughout this book, you will be asked to write as many words as you can remember from memory. This will help you to focus on what words look and sound like. Very soon, the words will start to roll off the end of your pencil!

The more you write, the better your spelling will be.

Short Vowels: a

a is a short, snappy sound.
Feel the corners of your mouth stretch as you say these words:
***a**nt, **a**xe, **a**pple, c**a**t, fl**a**g, scr**a**tch.*

SEE & SAY

at	bag	pack	plant	smack
cat	rag	sack	grant	track
am	ran	flag	damp	flash
jam	can	drag	stamp	crash

Nouns name the people and things in our world.
A **singular noun** names one person or thing.
A **plural noun** names more than one. To make a noun plural, we add **-s** most of the time. *Examples: 1 dog, 2 dogs; 1 boy, 2 boys; 1 toy, 2 toys*

1 Write these nouns in plural form.

cat	____________	flag	____________	sack	____________
plant	____________	track	____________	rag	____________
stamp	____________	bag	____________	can	____________

Add **-ing** and **-ed** to **verbs** to show when things are happening.
*Examples: Jill is pack**ing** her bag.* (NOW) *Jill pack**ed** her bag.* (PAST)

2 Add -ing or -ed to complete the verbs in bold.

Jan is **stamp**_______ her feet.

Mum **pack**_______ my lunch for school.

The farmers are **plant**_______ wheat.

A car **crash**_______ into a tree.

I am **go**____ to school.

c and k go together at the end of a word. They are the kissing cousins!
sma**ck**

LOOK & LEARN

I me he we she is are

TARGETING SPELLING 2 © PASCAL PRESS ISBN 9781925490206

Pronouns take the place of nouns. *Jack – he; Jill – she; horse – it; bird – it.* **Jack** has a **horse**. ***He*** rides ***it*** every day. **Jill** has a **bird**. ***She*** calls ***it*** Casper.

3 Choose a pronoun (I, me, he, she, we) to complete each sentence.

Tim has a pet puppy. ______ takes him for a walk every day.

Sam gave Sally and ______ a bunch of flowers.

My sister and ______ are twins. ______ have black hair.

Julie said ______ would lend ______ her pencil.

Rhyming words end in the same sound. *Examples: bag, rag, tag, wag, flag*. Rhyming words make it easy to learn many other words.

4 Complete this table of rhyming words.

cat	pack
f	b
h	t
r	r
b	tr
s	qu

MEMORY TRAINING

Read the words in each list two times. How many words can you remember? Write them in your notebook. Check and write your scores here.

....

q and u are best friends. They are always together.
quick, queen, quit

Compound words have two word parts, like this:

sun	shine

pan	cake

grand	mother

5 Write these compound words by joining the word parts.

back + pack backpack

flag + pole ______

flash + light ______

sun + hat ______

hand + bag ______

track + suit ______

Short Vowels: e

e is a short, snappy sound.
It is the sound you feel in the back of your throat when you say:
egg, elf, elephant and *get, rest, stretch.*

SEE & SAY

let	bed	fell	them	deck
get	red	shell	then	wreck
men	peg	went	pest	send
ten	leg	tent	west	bend

When you see **wr**, do NOT sound the **w**.
wrap = rap;
wreck = reck;
wring = ring

1 Name the pictures.

2 Write these nouns in plural form.

pet ________	shell ________	leg ________
peg ________	bed ________	pest ________
step ________	desk ________	shed ________

3 Add an ending to the verbs in bold. Choose from -s, -ing and -ed.

Ty is **bend**_____ down to tie his shoelaces.

Mum **let**_____ me help her put out the clothes.

The ship was **wreck**_____ in the storm last night.

Jane is **send**_____ Christmas cards to all her friends.

LOOK & LEARN

you your yours was were the

TARGETING SPELLING 2 © PASCAL PRESS ISBN 9781925490206

Some **verbs** have a special past time form. *Examples: I **see** you. (NOW) I **saw** you. (PAST) I **run** fast. (NOW) I **ran** fast. (PAST)*

4 Change the verb in each sentence to past time. Choose a word from the box and write it on the line.

went
fell
bent
ran
got

Ty **bends** down to tie his shoelaces. ______________

They **get** home at four o'clock. ______________

The boys **go** to football training. ______________

Leaves **fall** off the trees. ______________

Toby **runs** to catch the school bus. ______________

5 Choose a pronoun (you, your, yours) to complete the sentences.

Is this pencil ______________?

Put ______________ lunch in ______________ lunchbox.

Did ______________ help ______________ mum put out the clothes?

I'd like ______________ to come and bring all ______________ friends.

6 Write the rhyming words from these word wheels.

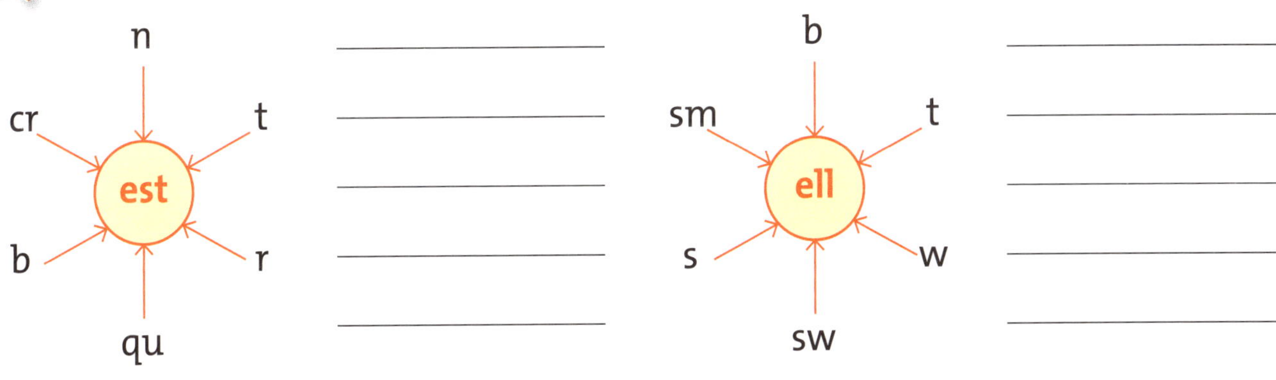

MEMORY TRAINING

Read the words in each list two times. How many words can you remember? Write them in your notebook. Check and write your scores here. ....

7 Add vowels to mend the broken words. Choose from a and e.

We **sw__m** between the **fl__gs** at the beach.

We found **seash__lls** on the **d__mp s__nd**.

Dan **f__ll** off his bike and cut his **l__g**.

We'll **p__ck** our food and a **t__nt**, and **c__mp** by the river.

TARGETING SPELLING 2 © PASCAL PRESS ISBN 9781925490206

UNIT 3

Short Vowels: i

i is a short, snappy sound.
It is the sound you hear when you bring your shoulders up to your ears, as you say: *in, it, ill* and *pig, slip, brick.*

SEE & SAY

zip	pig	hill	slip	list
lip	dig	will	trip	fist
sit	did	pink	trick	skin
knit	lid	sink	brick	thin

1 Name the pictures.

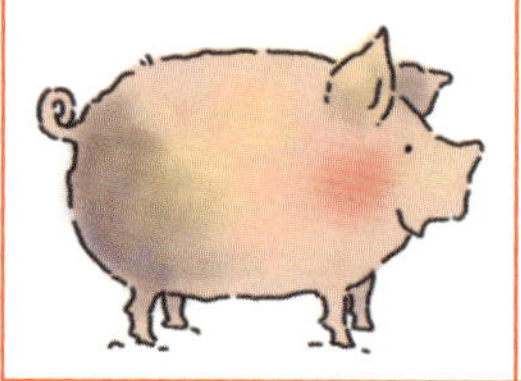				

DOUBLING RULE

We add **-ing** and **-ed** to most **verbs** to show *present* and *past* time.
When there is only *one* consonant after a short vowel, **double** that consonant before you add **-ing** or **-ed**.
Examples: hop, hopping, hopped.
If there are already *two* consonants after the short vowel, just add an ending. *Examples: flash, flashing, flashed; test, testing, tested; spell, spelling, spelled.*

2 Use the doubling rule to write the verbs in present and past time.

	Add -ing	Add -ed
zip	zipping	zipped
trick		
knit		
list		
trip		

LOOK & LEARN

go give do for

TARGETING SPELLING 2 © PASCAL PRESS ISBN 9781925490206

3 Add an ending to the words in bold. Choose from -s, -ing and -ed.

UNIT 3

Tony **trip**_____ and fell across the **finish**_____ line.

Mum **knit**_____ a beanie and a scarf for me.

The teacher **list**_____ our names on the board.

The farmer has **pig**_____, **hen**_____, **duck**_____, **cow**_____ and sheep.

Adjectives are describing words. *Examples: pink, red, fat, thin, wet, cold.* Sometimes, we build adjectives by adding **-y** to words. *Example: sand**y**.*

4 Add -y to build adjectives.

hill___	trick___	wind___
mess___	mist___	smell___
hand___	silk___	stick___

5 Complete this table of rhyming words.

zip	**brick**
t	l
s	t
d	s
dr	st
gr	qu

MEMORY TRAINING

Read the words in each list two times. How many words can you remember? Write them in your notebook. Check and write your scores here.

....

6 Choose a special past time verb from the box to write beside each present time verb.

ran did went fell dug gave sat got

run ran	fall	do	go
give	dig	sit	get

Don't mix up **four** and **for**.

Four is a number (4). *Example: I have **four** pets.*

For begins a phrase.
Examples: for you; for a day; for a swim; for Mum.

Short Vowels: o

o is a short, snappy sound.
It is the sound where you make your mouth round like a letter O when you say:
off, odd, orange and *pot, stop, frost.*

SEE & SAY

hot	odd	toss	lost	flop
pot	rod	boss	frost	crop
hop	lock	stop	clock	spot
top	rock	drop	block	trot

1 Write these nouns in plural form.

pot ____________ rock ____________ spot ____________
block ____________ rod ____________ crop ____________
cot ____________ pond ____________ clock ____________

2 Add -ing and -ed to these verbs. Use the doubling rule.

	Add -ing	Add -ed
hop	hopping	hopped
rock		
stop		
toss		
spot		
flop		

3 Write four more words that rhyme with each word.

hop ____________ ____________ ____________ ____________
cat ____________ ____________ ____________ ____________
pin ____________ ____________ ____________ ____________
nest ____________ ____________ ____________ ____________

LOOK & LEARN

here there where see saw

TARGETING SPELLING 2 © PASCAL PRESS ISBN 9781925490206

Complete this table of rhyming words.

hot	lock
c	s
d	st
n	fl
l	kn
sh	sh

When you see **kn**, do NOT sound the **k**.
knit = nit;
knot = not;
knock = nock

MEMORY TRAINING

Read the words in each list two times. How many words can you remember? Write them in your notebook. Check and write your scores here.

....

Colour the correct word in the brackets.

I [seen saw] a bus at the bus stop.

I don't know [where were] I lost my hat.

I'm going to the shop [four for] an ice cream.

I wear a [red read] school cap.

Syllables are the chunks of sounds you can hear in a word. **Dog** has ✋ syllable, **rab bit** has ✋✋, **lem on ade** has ✋✋✋ and **hel i cop ter** has ✋✋✋✋. How many **syllables** are in your first name? ____

Join the syllables to say each word. Draw a line from the word to the picture.

pig let   pos sum   rock et   let ter   pot a to

Add -y to build adjectives.

boss____	rock____	frost____
milk____	moss____	risk____

How many words can you remember?

Go back and choose any *See and Say* list. Read through it twice, focusing on how the words look and sound. Write as many words as you can remember in your notebook. Check how many you have written correctly and enter your score here.

Short Vowels: u

u is a short, snappy sound.
It is the sound you hear when you drop your jaw, as you say: ***up, us, under*** and ***rug, junk, truck.***

(Place your hands under your jaw like a letter **u**. Lower your hands as you lower your jaw.)

SEE & SAY

sun	but	duck	truck	club
run	cut	luck	stuck	grub
mug	cub	jump	crust	junk
rug	tub	lump	trust	bunk

1 Name the pictures.

2 Write these nouns in plural form.

grub ____________ mug ____________ crust ____________
truck ____________ cub ____________ duck ____________
lump ____________ bunk ____________ tub ____________

DOUBLING RULE

When there is only *one* consonant after a short vowel, **double** that consonant before you add **-y**. *Examples: bag, baggy; fun, funny.*
If there are already *two* consonants after the short vowel, just add **-y**. *Examples: dust, dusty; wind, windy; jump, jumpy; boss, bossy; frost, frosty*

3 Use the doubling rule to add -y to build adjectives.

sun ____________ luck ____________ flop ____________
crust ____________ run ____________ skin ____________
grub ____________ trust ____________ stick ____________

LOOK & LEARN

all my her hers of off

TARGETING SPELLING 2 © PASCAL PRESS ISBN 9781925490206

4 Join the word parts to say the compound words. Write the words under the pictures.

sun shine   bath tub   butter cup   pad lock   lip stick

5 Choose a special past time verb from the box to write beside each present time verb.

swam   stuck   lost   gave   was   ran   were   did

run	stick	are	swim
is	do	lose	give

6 Write the rhyming words on this wall of bricks.

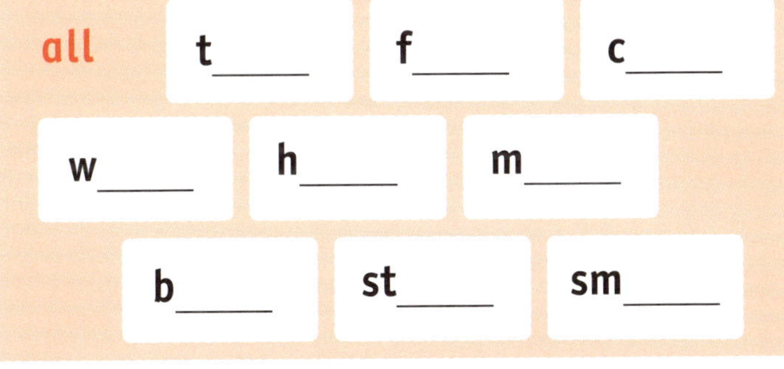

MEMORY TRAINING

Read the words on the wall two times. How many words can you remember? Write them in your notebook. Check and write your score here.

....

7 Add -ing and -ed to these verbs. Use the doubling rule.

	Add -ing	Add -ed
duck	ducking	ducked
jump		
trust		
hum		
tug		
hunt		

Consonant Digraphs: sh, ch

sh: When we put **s** and **h** together, they make only one sound — the sound you hear in ***shop, ship, shut, wish, fish*** and ***dish***.
ch: When we put **c** and **h** together, they make only one sound — the sound you hear in ***chat, chop, chip, much*** and ***such***.

SEE & SAY

shop	wish	chop	fetch
ship	fish	chick	much
shut	crush	chin	such
shack	trash	chat	lunch
shed	brush	catch	bunch

1 Name the pictures.

To write nouns in their plural form, add **-s** most of the time.
Add **-es** to nouns that end in **s**, **x**, **sh** and **ch**.
Examples: bus, buses; fox, foxes; dish, dishes; match, matches

2 Use the rule above to write these nouns in plural form.

shop ______	ship ______	shack ______
lunch ______	chick ______	shed ______
wish ______	bunch ______	brush ______

LOOK & LEARN

yes no so want

TARGETING SPELLING 2 © PASCAL PRESS ISBN 9781925490206

WORD TRAPS

Don't mix up **want** and **went**.

If you **want** something, you would like to have it.
*Examples: I **want** an apple. Tim **wants** a banana.*

Went is a past time verb.
*Examples: We **went** to the beach. Jane **went** to the movies.*

3 Add an ending to the words in bold. Choose from -s, -es, -ing and -ed.

I am going **shop**________ with my dad.

Joe **brush**____ his teeth before he **go**____ to bed.

The cat **scratch**____ me with her sharp **claw**___ yesterday.

Mum bought six **apple**___ and two **bunch**____ of grapes.

I like **chat**______ to my **friend**___ at lunchtime.

4 Complete this table of rhyming words.

patch	itch
m	p
l	w
b	d
sn	st
scr	sw

MEMORY TRAINING

Read the words in each list two times. How many words can you remember? Write them in your notebook. Check and write your scores here.

....

DOUBLING RULE

When there is only *one* consonant after a short vowel, **double** that consonant before you add **-er**. *Example: shop, shopper.*
If there are already *two* consonants after the short vowel, just add **-er**. *Example: dust, duster*

5 Use the doubling rule to add -er to these words.

run ____________	catch ____________	jump ____________
chat ____________	bat ____________	swim ____________
send ____________	let ____________	but ____________

6 Add -y to build adjectives. Think about the doubling rule.

chat ____________	itch ____________	rag ____________
crunch ____________	fog ____________	chill ____________

UNIT 7

Word Endings: -er

Many words end in -er. This syllable sounds like uh when we say it. It is the sound that rolls off the end of the word. You will need to remember what these words *look* like.

SEE & SAY

dinner	gutter	over	winter
winner	chopper	under	summer
ladder	flipper	thunder	whisper
bitter	slipper	river	monster
butter	swimmer	shiver	hunger

1 Add an ending to the words in bold. Choose from -s, -ing, -ed and -y.

Cal is **shiver**____ in the cold winter wind.

Bella slid down the **slipper**____ slide.

Summer___ are hot and **winter**___ are cold.

Ben **whisper**_____ something to his friend.

2 Be a word builder by adding -er. Use the doubling rule.

crack_____	spin_____	drum_____	sit_____	dust_____
sing_____	stop_____	camp_____	knit_____	run_____

We add -er to show how two things compare with each other. We add -est to show how more than two things compare with each other. *Examples: big, bigger, biggest; fresh, fresher, freshest*

3 Add -er and -est to these adjectives. Use the doubling rule.

	Add -er	Add -est
fat		
thin		
sick		
hot		
long		

LOOK & LEARN

one	once
have	how

TARGETING SPELLING 2 © PASCAL PRESS ISBN 9781925490206

4 Join the word parts to make compound words.

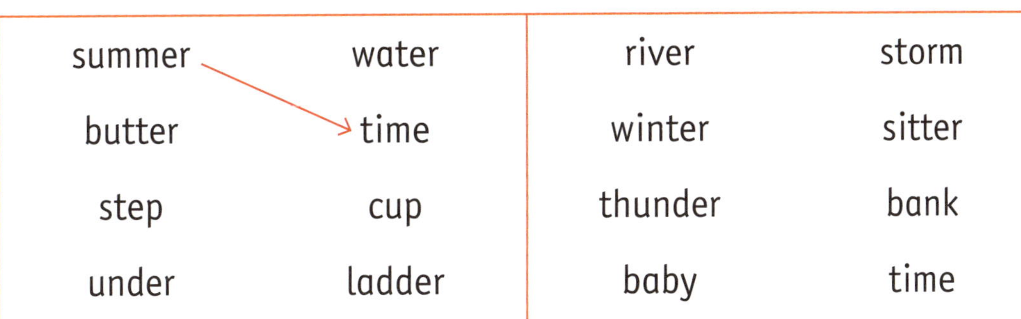

summer	water	river	storm
butter	time	winter	sitter
step	cup	thunder	bank
under	ladder	baby	time

5 Join the syllables to the word stem.

pat, clat, mut, lit, shel, splat → **ter**

Write the words here.	Add **-ed** here.
patter	pattered

6 Write a few sentences to continue this story. Draw your monster.

Once upon a time, in a deep, dark wood, there lived a hairy monster.

UNIT 8

Compound Words

A **compound word** is made by joining two words together.
Examples: ***sun*** *+ hat =* ***sun****hat;* ***book*** *+ shelf =* ***book****shelf*

SEE & SAY

backpack	sunhat	somehow	everything
padlock	matchbox	something	nobody
lipstick	matchstick	somewhere	nowhere
knockout	windmill	everywhere	myself
handbag	standstill	everyone	yourself

1 Choose a word from the *See and Say* list to complete each sentence.

E____________ in my class likes playing ball games.

The train came to a **s**______________ at the railway station.

I looked **e**______________ for my ball, but I didn't find it.

I would like a glass of milk and **s**______________ to eat.

The family lost **e**______________ in the fire.

2 Read these compound words.
Choose one word from each group and use them in sentences.

sun	set	water	fall	sea	side
sun	shine	water	hole	sea	shell
sun	flower	water	melon	sea	horse

1. ______________________________

2. ______________________________

3. ______________________________

LOOK & LEARN

very every out about

TARGETING SPELLING 2 © PASCAL PRESS ISBN 9781925490206

3 Add vowels (a, e, i, o, u) to mend the broken compound words.

Mum put her car keys in her **h__nd | b__g.**

She put on her **l__p | st__ck** and her pink **s__n | h__t.**

Jim took a **m__tch | st__ck** out of the **m__tch | b__x.**

I put my books and **l__nch | b__x** in my **b__ck | p__ck.**

4 Name the pictures. All words are compound words.

5 Colour the pairs of words that make a compound word. Use a different colour for each pair.

foot	egg	thunder	sun	week	rain
storm	end	ball	drops	shell	light

6 Choose a word part in the box to complete each compound word.

room side tops cakes suit

I put on a **track**________ to go for my morning jog.

Dale likes **cup**________ with pink icing.

My **bed** ________ is next to the **bath**________.

Magpies are nesting in the **tree**________.

Dylan rode very fast down the steep **hill**________.

How many words can you remember?

Go back and choose any *See and Say* list. Read through it twice, focusing on how the words look and sound. Write as many words as you can remember in your notebook. Check how many you have written correctly and enter your score here.

Term 1 Review

1 Write these nouns in plural form.

rag ____________	bunch ____________	shed ____________
plant ____________	crust ____________	lunch ____________
boss ____________	wish ____________	rock ____________

2 Name the pictures.

3 Add -y to form adjectives. *(Remember the spelling rules.)*

rock ____________	skin ____________	dust ____________
rag ____________	frost ____________	stick ____________
smell ____________	flop ____________	grub ____________

4 Colour the correct word.

I have [to two] sandwiches and [for four] plums in my lunchbox.

The children [want went] to go and play in the [send sand].

Jai lost his hat [something somewhere] in the park.

[Were Where] is the ball I [give gave] you?

5 Add -er to these words. *(Remember the spelling rules.)*

jump_____	run_____	but_____
shop_____	pot_____	camp_____
catch_____	lock_____	knit_____
sink_____	slip_____	sing_____

TARGETING SPELLING 2 © PASCAL PRESS ISBN 9781925490206

6 Name the pictures *(Hint: All are compound words).*

7 Add endings to these verbs to show present (now) and past tense. *(Remember the spelling rules.)*

Add -s or -es		Add -ing		Add -ed	
crunch		hum		shiver	
chop		wish		jump	
toss		sit		slam	
fetch		hop		spot	

8 Complete this table of present (now) and special past time verbs.

Now	Past
do	
run	
bend	
fall	

Now	Past
	saw
	got
	dug
	went

9 Circle the spelling mistakes. Write the correct words on the lines.

I had crakers and cheese, and for olives. ____________ ____________

Two trucks crasht and blokt the street. ____________ ____________

Sumone whisped my name. ____________ ____________

The swimma has goggles and flipers. ____________ ____________

10 Write rhyming words.

can	pest	pink	hop	must	catch

UNIT 9

Long Vowels: ā (a _ e)

The vowel a has a short sound (*cat*), and a long sound (*cake*).
A long **a** (ā) has the same sound as its name, and often follows the pattern, a _ e. *Examples: cake, tale, game, shade.* The **e** on the end is silent.

SEE & SAY

game	save	race	plane	plate
same	cave	face	crane	skate
tale	make	trace	shape	snake
sale	take	place	scrape	brake

Choose a word from the *See and Say* list to complete the sentences.

Come over to my **p**__________ for a **g**__________ of cricket.

Did you **t**__________ the last biscuit off the **p**__________?

Jack won the **g**__________ of **S**__________**s** and Ladders.

I will **r**__________ you across the ice on my **s**__________**s**.

Complete this table of rhyming words.

gate	game
l	n
m	t
h	c
r	l
gr	fl

WORD TRAPS

Don't mix up **tale** and **tail**.

*Examples: A **tale** is a story.*
*A cat has a **tail**.*

Don't mix up **sale** and **sail**.

*Examples: You buy things at a **sale**.*
*You **sail** a boat.*
*Wind fills the **sails** and pushes the boat through the water.*

Don't mix up **plane** and **plain**.

*Examples: You would fly in a **plane**.*
*You would eat **plain** food.*

LOOK & LEARN

boy
girl
two
first

TARGETING SPELLING 2 © PASCAL PRESS ISBN 9781925490206

UNIT 9

3 Name the pictures. All have the pattern a _ e.

THE 'e' RULE

When verbs end in **e**, drop the **e** before adding **-ing**, **-ed** and **-y**.
Examples: wave, waving, waved, wavy
Just add **-s** to show present time (*waves*).

4 Use the e rule to complete this table of verbs.

	Add -s	Add -ing	Add -ed
save	saves	saving	saved
scrape			
brake			
place			
skate			

5 Use the e rule to add -y to build adjectives.

shake ____________ shade ____________ race ____________

lace ____________ laze ____________ scale ____________

6 Write the rhyming words on this wall of bricks.

make

b____ r____ c____ w____ sh____

l____ f____ dr____ qu____

7 Choose a special past time verb from the box to write beside each present time verb.

ran gave shook made did woke was took

run ran	make	give	take
shake	is	wake	do

UNIT 10

Long Vowels: ī (i – e)

The vowel **i** has a short sound (*him*), and a long sound (*like*).
A long **i** (ī) has the same sound as its name, and often follows the pattern, **i – e**. *Examples: time, white, five, wide.* The **e** on the end is silent.

SEE & SAY

ride	like	ice	shine	slide
side	bike	rice	spine	glide
kite	fine	price	smile	stripe
white	line	twice	while	strike

1 Write these nouns in plural form.

bike ____________ stripe ____________ smile ____________

price ____________ line ____________ kite ____________

THE 'e' RULE

When verbs end in **e**, drop the **e** before adding **-ing**, **-ed** and **-y**.
Examples: ice, icing, iced, icy. Just add **-s** to show present time (*ices*).

2 Add endings to the words in bold. Choose from -s, -ing, -ed and -y.

ride Jed is ________________ his skateboard in the park.

smile My friend ________________ when she sees me.

shine Jess stepped out in her new ________________ red shoes.

slide We like ________________ in the slippery, wet mud.

glide We ______________ across the ice on our skates.

3 Write three rhyming words for each of these words.

ride	fine	ice	stripe
t	n	n	r
w	p	sl	p
h	d	sp	w

MEMORY TRAINING

Read the words in each list two times. How many words can you remember? Write them in your notebook. Check and write your scores here.

....

....

LOOK & LEARN

look his our ours their theirs

TARGETING SPELLING 2 © PASCAL PRESS ISBN 9781925490206

UNIT 10

4 Name the pictures. All have the pattern i_e.

5	[dice]	[kite]	9	[mice]

5 Colour the correct word in the brackets.

The books are [our ours] and the comics are [his her].

Billy was the [fast first] boy [to two] cross the line.

I [lick like] lizards, but not [snakes snacks].

Ellis [ride rode] his bike around the park [twice two].

6 Add vowels to mend the broken words. Choose between a and i.

Many children r__**de** their b__**kes** to school.

Danny has m__**de** a paper k__**te** with a long tail.

Timmy l__**kes** to sl__**de** down the slippery sl__**de**.

Mum put a sl__**ce** of birthday c__**ke** on my pl__**te**.

Note the long vowel pattern:
a_e
i_e

7 Write in the missing words.

You would **r**__________ a horse.

You would **s**__________ on ice.

A **b**__________ has two wheels.

Tennis is a fast **g**__________.

You cut your food with a **kn**__________.

The sun **s**__________ on fine days.

8 Choose a special past time verb from the box to write beside each present time verb.

ran struck bit slid shone rose rode hid

run ran	bite	hide	ride
slide	rise	strike	shine

9 Join the word parts to make compound words.

skate →	shine	bag	show
back	board	side	time
sun	bone	summer	pipes

Long Vowels: ō (o _ e)

The vowel **o** has a short sound (*hot*), and a long sound (*home*). A long **o** (ō) has the same sound as its name, and often follows the pattern, **o _ e**. *Examples: rose, bone, note, those*. The **e** on the end is silent.

SEE & SAY

rode	rose	wrote	broke	slope
code	nose	note	spoke	scope
bone	woke	stone	drove	those
cone	poke	throne	stove	close

When you see **wr**, do NOT sound the **w**.
wrap = rap;
wreck = reck;
wrote = rote

1 Write these nouns in plural form.

nose ______________ note ______________ rose ______________

bone ______________ cone ______________ stove ______________

When verbs end in **e**, drop the **e** before adding **-ing**, **-ed** and **-y**.
Examples: poke, poking, poked, poky.
Just add **-s** to show present time *(pokes)*.

2 Complete this table of verbs.

	Add -s	Add -ing	Add -ed
poke			
close			
drone			
doze			

3 Write three rhyming words for each of these words.

woke	bone	rose	slope
j	l	h	r
ch	dr	p	h
sm	ph	ch	m

MEMORY TRAINING

Read the words in each list two times. How many words can you remember? Write them in your notebook. Check and write your score here.

....

LOOK & LEARN

open over cold these

TARGETING SPELLING 2 © PASCAL PRESS ISBN 9781925490206

UNIT 11

4 Add -y to build adjectives. Use the e rule.

smoke ______ rose ______

bone ______ stone ______

nose ______ doze ______

5 Choose two of the adjectives above and use them in sentences.

______.

______.

6 Change the verb in each sentence to past time. Choose a word from the box and write it on the line.

drove
rose
wrote
rode
woke

They **ride** skateboards in the park. ______

I **wake** early on Sunday. ______

Dad **drives** his car to work. ______

We **write** to each other often. ______

They **rise** early every morning. ______

7 Add vowels to mend the broken words. Choose between a, i and o.

My n__**me** is Jack and I'm n__**ne** years old.

Bart r__**de** his b__**ke** to the football g__**me**.

I wr__**te** a funny t__**le** about a dancing sn__**ke**.

Dad dug a h__**le** with his sp__**de**.

Note the long vowel pattern:
a–e i–e
o–e

8 Write the missing words.

A king sits on a **th**______. Mum cooks on a **st**______.

A **r**______ is a pretty flower. You open and **cl**______ a door.

You smell with your **n**______. Dogs like to chew on **b**______.

Ice cream can be in a **c**______. You water gardens with a **h**______.

WORD TRAPS

Don't mix up rode and road.

Rode is a special past time verb.

*Examples: Today, I **ride** my bike. Yesterday, I **rode** my bike.*

*I **rode** my bike along the dusty **road**.*

UNIT 12

Long Vowels: ū (u _ e)

The vowel **u** has a short sound (*cup*), and a long sound (***use***).
A long **u (ū)** has the same sound as its name, and often follows the pattern, **u _ e**. *Examples: **rude, cube, use, flute***

SEE & SAY

cube	mule	brute	pure	rude
tube	rule	chute	cure	crude
tune	cute	use	duke	fuse
dune	flute	amuse	fluke	refuse

1 Write these nouns in plural form.

tube ______________ dune ______________ cube ______________

flute ______________ duke ______________ mule ______________

When verbs end in **e**, drop the **e** before adding **-ing** and **-ed**.
Examples: use, using, used.
Just add **-s** to show present time (*uses*).

2 Add endings to the words in bold to complete the sentences.

amuse The teacher read an __________________ story to the class.

rule Use your __________________ to draw a line 2 cm long.

refuse Tilly __________________ to jump in the deep end of the pool.

tune Lisa can play many __________________ on her flute.

cure Doctor Locke has __________________ many people of an illness.

3 Draw a line to match each word and picture.

mule parachute tube flute cube

LOOK & LEARN

talk walk with what

TARGETING SPELLING 2 © PASCAL PRESS ISBN 9781925490206

4 Add vowels to mend the broken words. Choose between a, i, o and u.

Note the long vowel pattern:
a–e i–e
o–e u–e

Mum __**sed** a **kn**__**fe** to cut the **c**__**ke** into **sl**__**ces**.

We **gl**__**ded** across the __**ce** on our **sk**__**tes**.

He is a bully and a **br**__**te** and **r**__**de** to everyone.

We saw a **sn**__**ke** in the sand **d**__**nes**.

I __**sed** my **r**__**ler** to draw a **l**__**ne** across the **p**__**ge**.

5 Add -er to say who these people are.

Example: One who dances is a dancer.

One who **rides** is a ____________.

One who **bakes** is a ____________.

One who **dives** is a ____________.

One who **writes** is a ____________.

One who **skates** is a ____________.

One who **rules** is a ____________.

One who **drives** is a ____________.

One who **jokes** is a ____________.

Adverbs say more about verbs. **-ly** is added to words to make adverbs.
*Examples: She spoke **softly**. She spoke **loudly**. She spoke **slowly**. She spoke **quickly**.*

When a word ends in **e**, do NOT drop the **e** before adding **-ly**.
*Examples: She spoke **rudely**. She spoke **wisely**.*

6 Use this rule to build adverbs by adding -ly.

fine ____________ like ____________ game ____________

close ____________ late ____________ cute ____________

7 Write the missing words.

A **c**____________ has six sides.

Toothpaste is in a **t**____________.

Music is played on a **fl**____________.

A **d**____________ is a sand hill.

A **m**____________ is like a donkey.

A **t**____________ is played on a flute.

A doctor **c**____________ sick people.

A water slide is a water **ch**____________.

How many words can you remember?

Go back and choose any *See and Say* list. Read through it twice, focusing on how the words look and sound. Write as many words as you can remember in your notebook. Check how many you have written correctly and enter your score here.

Compound Words

A compound word is made by joining two words together.
Examples: bed + time = ***bedtime****; book + case =* ***bookcase***

SEE & SAY

bedtime	**home**work	**out**side	**drive**way
lifetime	**home**land	**in**side	**take**away
lifeline	**fire**man	**under**line	**milk**shake
lifesaver	**fire**place	**summer**time	**snake**skin
notepaper	**fire**side	**pen**knife	**lines**man

Choose a compound word from the *See and Say* list to complete the sentences.

Dad always reads me a story at **b**________________.

We go swimming at the beach in the **s**________________.

I'd like to be a **f**________________ and fight fires.

Tanya had a chocolate **m**________________ and a cupcake.

We play **i**________________ on wet days.

Colour the pairs of words that make a compound word. Use a different colour for each pair.

play	skate	note	sun	side	race
book	show	time	track	shine	board

Draw a line to match a compound word and a picture.

sandcastle **thunder**storm **cup**cake **water**melon **sun**flower

LOOK & LEARN

some water after down

TARGETING SPELLING 2 © PASCAL PRESS ISBN 9781925490206

Using the word parts in the box, write six compound words.

fire	water	fly	side	light
out	sea	fall	sun	butter

________________ ________________ ________________

________________ ________________ ________________

5 Complete each compound word. Use the clues to help you.

sea__________	found on the beach
note__________	something to write on
summer__________	the hot part of the year
in__________	in the house
wind__________	it pumps water
no__________	not one person

Unscramble the compound words. Begin each word part with the letter in bold.

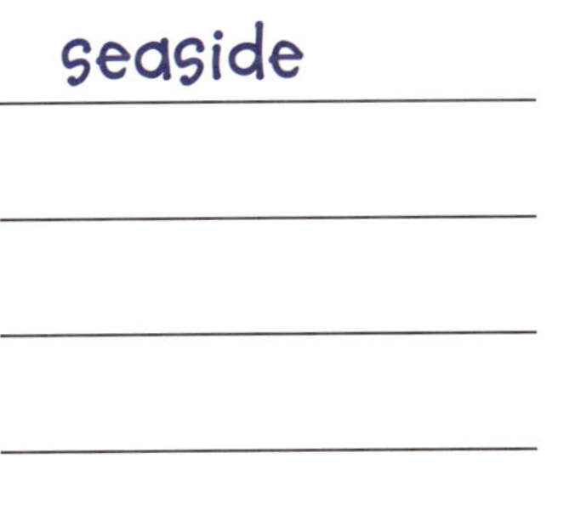

the beach	e**s**a i**s**de	seaside
worn on the lips	ip**l** **s**itkc	__________
he fights fires	i**f**er a**m**n	__________
during the day	ay**d** **t**eim	__________
not in the house	**o**tu d**s**ie	__________

Join the word parts to make compound words.

pop	ball	corn	pen
door	hill	egg	flakes
net	corn	book	shell
up	bell	pig	case

TARGETING SPELLING 2 © PASCAL PRESS ISBN 9781925490206

UNIT 14

Word Endings: y

Words that end in the letter **y** are **nouns**, **adjectives** or **verbs**. In this list, the words are all nouns.

SEE & SAY

day	monkey	baby	jelly
toy	chimney	body	gully
boy	trolley	lady	party
key	valley	buddy	family
donkey	jockey	country	fairy

1 Name the pictures.

THE 'y' RULE

To write the plural of **nouns** ending in **y**, follow these simple rules:

1 If the letter before the **y** is a vowel, just add **-s**.
Examples: boys, keys

2 If the letter before the **y** is not a vowel, change **y** to **i** and add **-es**.
Examples: baby, babies; lady, ladies

2 Use the y rule to write these words in plural form.

toy	______________	party	______________
gully	______________	valley	______________
body	______________	country	______________
jockey	______________	day	______________
family	______________	chimney	______________

LOOK & LEARN

done put pull push

TARGETING SPELLING 2 © PASCAL PRESS ISBN 9781925490206

Colour the pairs of words that make a compound word. Use a different colour for each pair.

lady	baby	day	Sun	key	boy
time	ring	bug	friend	sitter	day

Look for these nouns ending in y in the word search.

candy
ferry
bay
pantry
nappy
curry

l	t	r	b	h	n
y	d	n	a	c	a
k	l	f	y	u	p
f	p	m	s	r	p
p	a	n	t	r	y
f	e	r	r	y	x

Circle the spelling mistakes. Write the correct words on the lines.

Dad gave me a packet of lollys. ____________________

Smoke is coming from a tall chimny. ____________________

The jockies are riding race horses. ____________________

Jenny wore a wite party hat. ____________________

The babys are playing with soft toys. ____________________

Spell the missing words.

I asked Sally to come to my birthday **p**__________.

You will need a **k**__________ to lock the door.

There are two girls and two boys in my **f**__________.

Mum put bread and milk in a shopping **tr**__________.

Someb__________ is knocking on my door.

UNIT 15

Visual Patterns: igh, y

Words with the letters **igh** are very old. We don't hear the **gh**, but it has become trapped in the spelling. You will need to remember what these words *look* like. The letter **y** can be a vowel or a consonant. Here it has the long vowel sound **ī**.

SEE & SAY

high	night	right	my	try
sight	knight	fright	by	dry
light	might	bright	fly	shy
tight	fight	slight	cry	why

Choose a word from the *See and Say* list to complete the sentences.

A bird is flying ________________ above the treetops.

I got a ________________ when the door slammed shut.

I'm reading a book about a ________________ who fights a dragon.

I hung my wet clothes on the line to ________________.

Last ________________, the moon was very ________________.

WORD TRAPS

Don't mix up **night** and **knight**.

*Examples: You sleep at **night**. It is dark at **night**.*

*In olden days, a **knight** was a man who would fight for his king.*

When you see **kn**, do NOT sound the **k**. ***knit** = nit; **knot** = not*

Write the compound words from the word wheel. Make each compound word *end* with the word **light**.

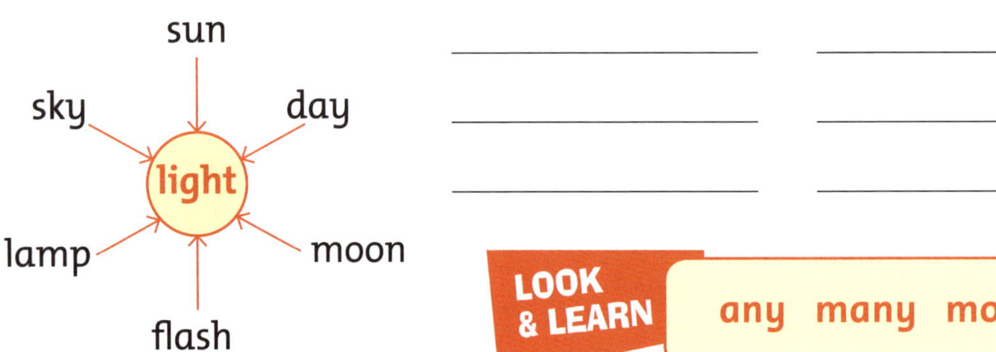

________________ ________________

________________ ________________

________________ ________________

LOOK & LEARN

any many more most

TARGETING SPELLING 2 © PASCAL PRESS ISBN 9781925490206

3 Colour the pairs of words that make a compound word. Use a different colour for each pair.

high	over	night	light	dragon	eye
clothes	house	way	sight	night	fly

To add endings to verbs ending in **y**, follow these simple rules:

1 Add **-ing** to verbs ending in **y**. *Examples: play**ing**, carry**ing***

2 If the letter before the **y** is a vowel, just add **-s**.
*Examples: play**s**, play**ed***

3 If the letter before the **y** is not a vowel, change **y** to **i** and add **-es**.
*Examples: tr**y**, tr**ies**, tr**ied***

4 Complete this table of verbs. (* = *special past time verbs*)

	Add -s / -es	Add -ing	Add -ed
try	tries	trying	tried
cry			
fry			
fly			* flew
buy			* bought

5 Write a letter in each box to spell the missing words.

I write with my ______ hand.

The knight rode off to ______ for his king.

The moon shone brightly last ______.

I saw a plane flying ______ in the sky.

It is time to put out the ______ and go to sleep.

6 Add -ly to build adverbs.

tight ____________________ light ____________________

slight ____________________ bright ____________________

night ____________________ shy ____________________

UNIT 16

Contractions

A contraction is the short form of two words.
An **apostrophe** marks where letters have been left out.

SEE & SAY

isn't	hasn't	don't	it's	I'm
aren't	haven't	won't	he's	you're
wasn't	didn't	couldn't	she's	they're
weren't	can't	wouldn't	that's	we're

Verbs followed by **not** are often written as contractions.
*Examples: do not = **don't**; has not = **hasn't**; will not = **won't***
An apostrophe is used in place of the letter o in *not*.

Colour the words and their matching contractions. Use a different colour for each pair.

was not	cannot	have not	are not	do not
haven't	don't	wasn't	can't	aren't

will not	has not	were not	could not	is not
couldn't	weren't	isn't	won't	hasn't

Verbs and their *pronoun* subjects are often written as **contractions**.
*Examples: I am = **I'm**; it is= **it's**; they are = **they're**; he will = **he'll***
An **apostrophe** is used in place of *the missing letter/s*.

Match the words and their contractions.

I am	you're	it is	they're
he is	we'd	we are	she'll
you are	I'm	you have	we're
they have	he's	they are	it's
we would	they've	she will	you've

TARGETING SPELLING 2 © PASCAL PRESS ISBN 9781925490206

LOOK & LEARN

other brother mother father

3 Write contractions for the words in bold.

I have not seen a wombat in the wild. ______________

My brother **cannot** do up his shoelaces yet. ______________

Do not jump on the bed. ______________

You are my very best friend. ______________

The train **will not** leave until six o'clock. ______________

WORD TRAPS

Don't mix up **it's** and **its**.

It's is a contraction for **it is**.

*Examples: **It's** a long way home and **it's** getting dark.*

Its is a pronoun showing ownership.

*Examples: A cat licks **its** paws. A bird flaps **its** wings.*

4 Colour the correct word in the brackets.

[Its It's] very cloudy today, and I think [its it's] going to rain.

You [can't couldn't] play in the mud in [you're your] school shoes.

[I'm I've] got new shoes, but [there they're] too big for me.

Jack [don't doesn't] know [we're where] he left his hat.

5 Use these contractions in sentences.

We're ____.

It's ____.

I don't ____.

He can't ____.

How many words can you remember?

Go back and choose any *See and Say* list. Read through it twice, focusing on how the words look and sound. Write as many words as you can remember in your notebook. Check how many you have written correctly and enter your score here.

1 Name the pictures.

2 Write these nouns in plural form.

branch ____________	price ____________	stone ____________
fireman ____________	party ____________	valley ____________
fly ____________	tune ____________	body ____________

3 Write the words of opposite meaning.

wet ____________	low ____________	day ____________
open ____________	under ____________	hot ____________
push ____________	winter ____________	inside ____________

4 Colour the correct word in the brackets.

[We're Where] going to the beach if [its it's] fine.

The [knight night] [road rode] off to fight for his king.

This is a [tale tail] about a dancing [snack snake].

Tim [don't doesn't] know if [there they're] coming to the park.

5 Add -ly to form adverbs. (*Remember the spelling rules.*)

fine ____________	bright ____________	game ____________
close ____________	rude ____________	slight ____________
late ____________	quick ____________	like ____________

TARGETING SPELLING 2 © PASCAL PRESS ISBN 9781925490206

Unit 1

1 cats, plants, stamps, flags, tracks, bags, sacks, rags, cans
2 stamping, packed, planting, crashed, going
3 He, me, I, We, she, me
4 memory training: cat, fat, hat, rat, bat, sat; pack, back, tack, rack, track, quack
5 backpack, flagpole, flashlight, sunhat, handbag, tracksuit

Unit 2

1 shell, tent, bed, peg, ten
2 pets, pegs, steps, shells, beds, desks, legs, pests, sheds
3 bending, lets, wrecked, sending
4 bent, got, went, fell, ran
5 yours; your, your; you, your; you, your
6 memory training: nest, test, rest, quest, best, crest; bell, tell, well, swell, sell, smell
7 swam, flags; seashells, damp, sand; fell, leg; pack, tent, camp

Unit 3

1 pig, brick, fist, knit (knitting), lips
2 tricking, tricked; knitting, knitted; listing, listed; tripping, tripped
3 tripped, finishing; knitted; listed; pigs, hens, ducks, cows
4 hilly, messy, handy, tricky, misty, silky, windy, smelly, sticky
5 memory training: tip, sip, dip, drip, grip; lick, tick, sick, stick, quick
6 give gave; fall fell; dig dug; do did; sit sat; go went; get got

Unit 4

1 pots, blocks, cots, rocks, rods, ponds, spots, crops, clocks
2 rocking, rocked; stopping, stopped; tossing, tossed; spotting, spotted; flopping, flopped
3 hop: cop, crop, drop, flop, lop, mop, stop, shop, slop, top

cat: bat, brat, chat, fat, hat, mat, pat, rat, sat, spat, scat, vat

pin: bin, din, fin, shin, skin, spin, tin, thin, twin, win

nest: best, crest, jest, pest, quest, rest, test, vest, west

4 memory training: hot, cot, dot, not, lot, shot; lock, sock, stock, flock, knock, shock
5 saw, where, for, red
6 rocket, letter, potato, possum, piglet
7 bossy, milky, rocky, mossy, frosty, risky

Unit 5

1 sun, truck, duck, mug, jump
2 grubs, trucks, lumps, mugs, cubs, bunks, crusts, ducks, tubs
3 sunny, crusty, grubby, lucky, runny, trusty, floppy, skinny, sticky
4 lipstick, buttercup, bathtub, sunshine, padlock
5 run ran; is was; stick stuck; do did; are were; lose lost; swim swam; give gave
6 memory training: all, tall, fall, call, wall, hall, mall, ball, stall, small
7 jumping, jumped; trusting, trusted; humming, hummed; tugging, tugged; hunting, hunted

Unit 6

1 fish, ship, chick, shop, chop
2 shops, lunches, wishes, ships, chicks, bunches, shacks, sheds, brushes
3 shopping, brushes, goes, scratched, claws, apples, bunches, chatting, friends
4 memory training: patch, match, latch, batch, snatch, scratch; itch pitch, witch, ditch, stitch, switch
5 runner, chatter, sender, catcher, batter, letter, jumper, swimmer, butter
6 chatty, crunchy, itchy, foggy, raggy, chilly

Unit 7

1 shivering, slippery, Summers, winters, whispered (whispers)
2 cracker, singer, spinner, stopper, drummer, camper, sitter, knitter, duster, runner
3 fatter fattest; thinner thinnest; sicker sickest; hotter hottest; longer longest
4 summertime, buttercup, stepladder, underwater, riverbank, wintertime, thunderstorm, babysitter
5 mutter muttered; shelter sheltered; splatter splattered; litter littered; clatter clattered
6 writing activity

Unit 8

1 Everyone, standstill, everywhere, something, everything
2 writing activity
3 handbag, lipstick, sunhat, matchstick, matchbox, lunchbox, backpack
4 windmill, jellyfish, eggcup, goldfish, butterfly
5 football, eggshell, thunderstorm, sunlight, weekend, raindrops
6 tracksuit, cupcakes, bedroom, bathroom, treetops, hillside
7 memory training

Term 1 review

1 rags, plants, bosses, bunches, crusts, wishes, sheds, lunches, rocks
2 clock, shell, flag, brush, ladder, pig, slippers (shoes), fish, peg, duck
3 rocky, raggy, smelly, skinny, frosty, floppy, dusty, sticky, grubby
4 two, four; want, sand; somewhere; Where, gave
5 jumper, shopper, catcher, sinker, runner, potter, locker, slipper, butter, camper, knitter, singer
6 butterfly, lipstick, windmill, handbag, padlock
7 crunches, chops, tosses, fetches; humming, wishing, sitting, hopping; shivered, jumped, slammed, spotted
8 do did; run ran; bend bent; fall fell; see saw; get got; dig dug; go went
9 crackers, four; crashed, blocked; someone, whispered; swimmer, flippers
10 Examples: can, ran, fan, man, pan, ban, tan, gran, span, than

pest, nest, west, rest, test, crest, chest, quest, vest

pink, sink, wink, think, link, rink, drink, brink, stink

hop, top, pop, cop, lop, mop, crop, drop, flop, stop, slop

must, dust, rust, crust, trust, gust, bust

catch, match, patch, latch, batch, hatch, snatch, scratch, thatch

TARGETING SPELLING 2 © PASCAL PRESS ISBN 9781925490206

Unit 9

1 place, game, take, plate, game, Snakes, race, skates

2 gate, late, mate, hate, rate, grate; game, name, tame, came, lame, flame

3 gate, cake, spade, wave, whale

4 scrapes, scraping, scraped; brakes, braking, braked; places, placing, placed; skates, skating, skated

5 shaky, lacy, shady, lazy, racy, scaly

6 make, bake, rake, cake, wake, shake, lake, fake, drake, quake

7 shake shook; make made; is was; give gave; wake woke; take took; do did

Unit 10

1 bikes, prices, stripes, lines, smiles, kites

2 riding, smiles, shiny, sliding, glided

3 memory training: ride, tide, wide, hide; fine, nine, pine, dine; ice, nice, slice, spice; stripe, ripe, pipe, wipe

4 five, dice, kite, nine, mice

5 ours, his; first, to; like, snakes; rode, twice

6 ride, bikes, made, kite, likes, slide, slide, slice, cake, plate

7 ride, skate (slide), bike, game, knife, shines

8 slide slid; bite bit; rise rose; hide hid; strike struck; ride rode; shine shone

9 skateboard, backbone, sunshine, bagpipes, sideshow, summertime

Unit 11

1 noses, bones, notes, cones, roses, stoves

2 pokes, poking, poked; closes, closing, closed; drones, droning, droned; dozes, dozing, dozed

3 memory training: joke, choke, smoke; lone, drone, phone; hose, pose, chose; rope, hope, mope

4 smoky, bony, nosy, rosy, stony, dozy

5 writing activity

6 rode, woke, drove, wrote, rose

7 name, nine; rode, bike, game; wrote, tale, snake; hole, spade

8 throne, rose, nose, cone, stove, close, bones, hose

Unit 12

1 tubes, flutes, dunes, dukes, cubes, mules

2 amusing, ruler, refused, tunes, cured

3 picture matching exercise

4 used, knife, cake, slices; glided, ice, skates; brute, rude; snake, dunes; used, ruler, line, page

5 rider, diver, skater, driver, baker, writer, ruler, joker

6 finely, closely, likely, lately, gamely, cutely

7 cube, flute, mule, cures, tube, dune, tune, chute

Unit 13

1 bedtime, summertime, fireman, milkshake, inside

2 playtime, skateboard, notebook, sunshine, sideshow, racetrack

3 picture matching exercise

4 fireside, firelight, firefly, butterfly, waterfall, waterside, seaside, outside, sunlight, seawater

5 seashell (seaweed), notepaper (notebook), summertime, inside (indoors), windmill, nobody

6 seaside, lipstick, fireman, daytime, outside

7 doorbell, netball, uphill, cornflakes, eggshell, bookcase, pigpen

Unit 14

1 baby, fairy, key, jelly, donkey
2 toys, gullies, bodies, jockeys, families, parties, valleys, countries, days, chimneys
3 ladybug, babysitter, daytime, Sunday, keyring, boyfriend
4 word search
5 lollies, chimney, jockeys, white, babies
6 party, key, family, trolley, Somebody

Unit 15

1 high, fright, knight, dry, night, bright
2 sunlight, daylight, moonlight, flashlight, lamplight, skylight
3 highway, overnight, nightclothes, lighthouse, dragonfly, eyesight
4 cries, crying, cried; fries, frying, fried; flies, flying, flew; buys, buying, bought
5 right, fight, night, high, light
6 tightly, slightly, nightly, lightly, brightly, shyly

Unit 16

1 cannot-can't; have not-haven't; are not-aren't; do not-don't; will not-won't; has not-hasn't; were not-weren't; could not-couldn't; is not-isn't
2 he is-he's; you are-you're; they have-they've; we would-we'd; it is-it's; we are-we're; you have-you've; they are-they're; she will-she'll
3 I've, can't, Don't, You're, won't
4 It's, it's; can't, your; I've, they're; doesn't, where
5 writing activity

Term 2 review

1 bone, baby, kite, monkey, snake, fairy, rose, donkey, plane, bike
2 branches, firemen, flies, prices, parties, tunes, stones, valleys, bodies
3 dry, closed (shut), pull, high, over, summer, night, cold, outside
4 We're, it's; knight, rode; tale, snake, doesn't, they're
5 finely, closely, lately, brightly, rudely, quickly, gamely, slightly, likely
6 rules, ruling, ruled; cries, crying, cried; opens, opening, opened; fries, frying, fried; crashes, crashing, crashed
7 flew, woke, slid, rode, shone, hid, made
8 stony, sandy, hilly, mighty, rosy, icy, funny, spicy, baggy
9 babies, cried; racing, bike; dries, hanging; ladies, shiny; plane, high

Unit 17

1 laid, rain, hail, tail, sail
2 nails, pains, sails, tails, rails
3 main, bail, pail, bait, paid, aim, maid, raise
4 pail, laid, rails, raise, fail
5 hailed, baiting, worms, used, nails
6 matching exercise
7 sail, pane, come, whales, tail, mail
8 mailbox, raindrops, railway, paintbrush, fingernail, rainbow

Unit 18

1 paint, grain, grain, stain, drain
2 paid, laid, maid, raid, afraid
3 drains, draining, drained; trains, training, trained; trails, trailing, trailed; stains, staining, stained

TARGETING SPELLING 2 © PASCAL PRESS ISBN 9781925490206

4 snail, paint, train, chain, mail
5 complain: to grumble about things; explain: to make something easy to understand; painter: someone who paints things, an artist; container: anything you can put things in
6 picture matching exercise
7 hailstorm, sailboat, railroad, nailbrush, brainwave, rainwater

Unit 19

1 bay, play, stay, day, rays, way
2 plays, playing, played; stays, staying, stayed; sways, swaying, swayed; sprays, spraying, sprayed
3 playtime, playthings, playground, daytime, daylight, daybed
4 concept development
5 haystack, flyspray, daybreak, runway, takeaway, hairspray
6 play, today, rains; Trains, railway, said; clay, painted; sailing, bay; waiting, mail
7 day, pay, nail, lays, grains, tail, played, wait

Unit 20

1 knees, queens, sheets, sheep, creeks, feet
2 memory training: feed, seed, weed, heed, deed, reed, greed; deep, jeep, weep, peep, keep, creep, steep
3 meeting, feeds, collects, greedy, cakes, meets, friends, weekly, needed
4 do-did, see-saw; pay-paid; feed-fed; meet-met; bleed-bled; say-said; weep-wept
5 windscreen, beehive, sheepskin, weekend, weekdays, kneepads, sunscreen, beekeeper, Queensland
6 writing activity

Unit 21

1 sweet, street, sleep, sweep, speed
2 sweeping, swept; speeding, sped; bleeding, bled; freezing, froze
3 green, sheen; freeze, squeeze; bleed, breed; sleep, creep; sweet, fleet
4 speeding, streets, singing, sweetly, trees, keeps, freezer, Oranges, sweeter, lemons, feeling, sleepy
5 memory training: meet, feet, fleet, greet, sleet, tweet; feel, heel, peel, reel, kneel, wheel
6 sleepover, wheelchair, speedway, streetlight, greenkeeper, wheelbarrow, freeway, sleepwalk, treetops
7 writing activity

Unit 22

1 beaks, leaves, meals, beaches, teachers
2 beat, cheat, seat, bleat, neat, treat, heat, pleat
3 seal, beak, wheat, beach, leaf
4 teaching, leaves, really, healed, teacher
5 teapot, teacup, teatime, teaspoon; seashore, seaside, seashell, seaweed
6 horse, heel; meat, main; reel, creek; weak, sea
7 beans, peas, seeds, see, green, leaves, tree, seal, sleeping, beach, sweeping, leaves, street, sleepy, really

Unit 23

1 dream, east, clean, cream, least
2 peach, reach; read, bead; team, beam; lean, mean; sneak, creak
3 When, Why, Who, Which
4 dirty-clean; most-least; strong-weak; west-east; sour-sweet; shallow-deep
5 teacher, speaker, healer, streamers, freezer, sweeper, leader, sneakers
6 sneakers, teacher, freezer, streamers
7 seabird, shopkeeper, schoolteacher, seatbelt, mealtime, seafood, meatball, peanuts, seedpod
8 writing activity

Unit 24

1 rumble, middle, saddle, cuddle, candles
2 wiggling, tangled, prickly, rumbled, trickling
3 battle, rattle, rubble, hobble, nettle, paddle, cattle, bottle, juggle, ripple
4 tangles, tangling, tangled; wiggles, wiggling, wiggled; trickles, trickling, trickled; juggles, juggling, juggled
5 stumble, puddle, apple, bottle, tremble, rumble, paddle, middle, tangled, prickly
6 fondle, huddle, fiddle, bubble, tumble, scramble, crumple, topple, sample

Term 3 review

1 seal, sheep, kettle, wheat, candle, train, saddle, leaf, tree, snail
2 peaches, beasts, wheels, rails, grains, creeks, beans, handles, prickles, leaves, puddles, streams
3 tale, screen, meet, week, heal
4 freeze-froze, lay-laid, see-saw, sleep-slept, pay-paid, teach-taught, meet-met
5 new (young), fast, before, happy, above, clean, east, weak, least
6 trees, green, sea, week, creek, meal, peaches, cream, feeling, sleepy, clean, teeth
7 rains, raining, rained; sneezes, sneezing, sneezed; stays, staying, stayed; giggles, giggling, giggled; cleans, cleaning, cleaned
8 teaspoon, mailbox, beachhouse, streetlight, saddlebag, raincoat, weekend, seashell, handlebars
9 sailed, stream; should, before; Which, main; friend, middle

Unit 25

1 goat, foal, boat, load, goal
2 boats, roads, loads, goats, loaves, toads, goals, coats
3 road, toad, goals, loaves, coat
4 loan, groan, roam, foam, coal, shoal
5 loaded, loaves, floating, coats
6 boatshed, roadway, toadstool, overcoat, goatherd, goalkeeper, roadworks
7 writing activity

Unit 26

1 coasts, coaches, toasters, throats
2 coaches (coached), Mondays, poached, toasted, croaking, bleating, washed, hands, soapy
3 coach-bus; road-highway; boat-ship; coat-jacket; coast-shore; moan-groan
4 coach, coast, boat, poached, toast, throat
5 picture matching activity
6 goal, grown, coal, loan, towed
7 word search activity
8 moan, goal, foal (loaf), boat, coat, soak, soap, goat, load, loan

TARGETING SPELLING 2 © PASCAL PRESS ISBN 9781925490206

Unit 27

1 following, blowing, snowy, burrowing, throwing, snowballs, bows, arrows
2 snowball, snowman, snowstorm, snowflakes
3 deep-shallow; fast-slow; below-above; sweet-sour; sink-float; high-low
4 flow, blow, know, row, grow, bow, sow, snow
5 showtime, rowboat, showroom, blowhole, sideshow, rainbow, lawnmower, wheelbarrow
6 flown, sown, grown, known, blown

Unit 28

1 cars, arms, sparks, jars, parks
2 memory training: part, dart, smart, cart, start, chart
3 barked, car, shark, sharp, farmer, market, park, dark
4 shark, car, dart, jar, cart
5 before, below, because, begin, began, beside, beneath, belong, become, became; away, along, above, asleep, apart, among, again, about, awake, around
6 parked, sparkling, jarred, marked, barring
7 sparkle, barber, army, remark, dollar, farmer, market, darken, carpenter, collar

Unit 29

1 stars, marches, yards, guards, scarves
2 chart, harp, harsh, charm, snarl, carve
3 farmhouse, farmland, farmwork, farmyard; carport, carsick, carpet, cargo
4 archer, artist, partner, target, marble, startle, party, sharpen
5 startles, startling, startled, marches, marching, marched, guards, guarding, guarded, carves, carving, carved
6 marching, lines, started, marbles, looked, starry, archer, bows, arrows, guarding, ducks, hens
7 Example: blue, red, green, yellow, brown, purple
8 Example: Sunday, Monday, Tuesday, Wednesday, Thursday, Friday, Saturday
9 overboard, smartphone, armpit, headscarf, parkland, artwork, barnyard, dartboard, archway

Unit 30

1 horses, torches, stores, sports, horns
2 ford, cord, lord, sword; fort, port, sort, snort
3 scoreboard, storeroom, sportsground, thunderstorm, seashore, torchlight
4 storms, storming, stormed; scores, scoring, scored; stores, storing, stored; snores, snoring, snored
5 more, Most, most, more, more
6 core, horse, shore, short, horns, sports, wore, shorts, torch, store
7 writing activity

Unit 31

1 parrot, rocket, pumpkin, funnel, trumpet
2 puppets, buttons, napkins, jackets, kittens
3 hammer, stopper, butter, pepper, apple, mango, window, handle, number, lobster
4 reading/matching exercise
5 kennel, kitten, puppet, possum, jacket, carrot, coffee, parrot, trumpet, Saturday
6 crack/ers; chick/en; bis/cuits; yog/hurt; hon/ey; lem/on/ade; spag/het/ti; Veg/e/mite; choc/o/late; pot/a/toes

Unit 32

1 buy, week, hear, saw
2 plane, four, pail, meet, eight, two
3 been, creek, heel, steel, whale, made, waste, pane
4 memory training: past, fast, mast, last, cast; able, table, cable, fable, stable
5 plane, too, pale, weak, be, eight, rode, sea
6 reel, wore, know, sale, hear, mail. Answer: You rock-it.

Term 4 review

1 boat, funnel, carrot, shark, possum, trumpet, arrow, horse, star, rocket
2 goats, guards, torches, weeks, coaches, scarves, scores, planes, loaves, arms, shows, arches
3 fast-slow; soft-hard; light-dark; finish-start; high-low; strong-weak; long-short; near-far; sink-float
4 foal, horse, tale, toad, hear, road, grown, saw
5 beside, before, because, behind, begin
6 snows, snowing, snowed; marches, marching, marched; sparkles, sparkling, sparkled; bar, barring, barred
7 Tuesday, Wednesday, Thursday, Friday, Saturday, Sunday
8 it tore, it has torn; they grew, they have grown; it blew, it has blown
9 rollercoaster, rainbow, roadworks, headscarf, boatshed, goalposts, stagecoach, raincoat, racehorse

TARGETING SPELLING 2 © PASCAL PRESS ISBN 9781925490206

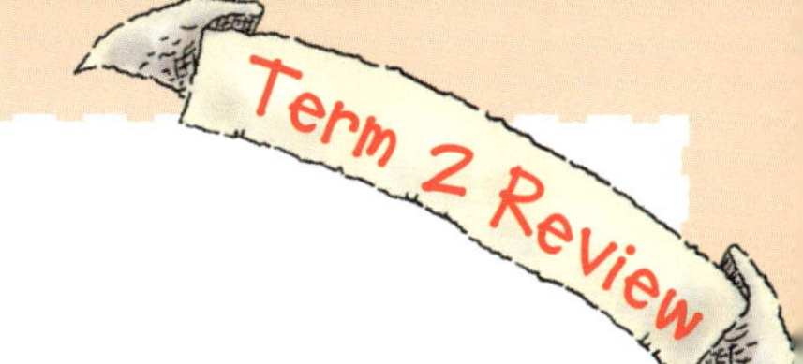

6 Complete this table of verbs. (*Remember the spelling rules.*)

	Add -s / -es	Add -ing	Add -ed
rule			
cry			
open			
fry			
crash			

7 Write the special past time of these verbs.

Present	Past
catch	caught
fly	
wake	
slide	

Present	Past
ride	
shine	
hide	
make	

8 Add -y to build adjectives. (*Remember the spelling rules.*)

stone ____________ might____________ fun ____________

sand ____________ rose ____________ spice ____________

hill ____________ ice ____________ bag ____________

9 Circle the spelling mistakes. Write the correct words on the lines.

The babys cryed when the door slammed. ____________ ____________

Tom is raceing downhill on his bick. ____________ ____________

The sun drys the sheets hangin on the line. ____________ ____________

The ladys wore shiney red shoes. ____________ ____________

A jet plain is flying hi in the sky. ____________ ____________

UNIT 17

Letter Teams: ai

The letters **ai** work together to make one sound — the long vowel sound ā, as in *rain (r **ai** n), tail (t **ai** l)* and *wait (w **ai** t)*. It is most often seen in the middle of a word.

SEE & SAY

rain	sail	nail	wail
pain	rail	fail	aid
tail	mail	hail	laid

1 Choose words from the *See and Say* list to complete the sentences.

The hen **l**__________ a big brown egg.

The storm brought **r**__________, **h**__________ and strong winds.

I made a kite with a long **t**__________.

The boat has one large **s**__________ and two small ones.

2 Write these nouns in plural form.

nail	pain	sail	tail	rail
________	________	________	________	________

3 Add **ai** to complete these words. Read the words aloud.

m____n	p____l	p____d	m____d
b____l	b____t	____m	r____se

4 Write a letter in each square to spell the missing words. Here are the clues.

Jack and Jill went up the hill to fetch a ______ of water.

The hen has ______ three brown eggs.

A train runs on ______.

He will ______ the flag to the top of the pole.

I hope I don't ______ my spelling test.

p				
l				
r				
r				
f				

LOOK & LEARN: come ask find people

TARGETING SPELLING 2 © PASCAL PRESS ISBN 9781925490206

Don't mix up **pain** and **pane**.
Examples:
***Pain** is the hurt you feel if you get injured or sick.*
*A **pane** is a sheet of glass in a window.*

Don't mix up **pail** and **pale**.
*Examples: A **pail** is a bucket.*
*Something **pale** is not very bright in colour.*

5 Add an ending to the words in bold. Choose from -s, -ing and -ed.

We **hail**______ a bus to take us to the shopping mall.

The boys are **bait**______ their fishing hooks with **worm**______.

Dad **use**______ a hammer and some **nail**______ to fix the fence.

6 Join the words to their correct pictures.

male	mail	bales	bails

7 Circle the correct word in the brackets.

Jack Trad wants to [sale sail] his boat around the world.

Ty threw the cricket ball hard and broke a window [pane pain].

The people have [came come] to watch the [whales wails].

A fox has a long, bushy [tail tale].

A birthday card from my grandma came in the [male mail].

8 Join the word parts to write these compound words.

mail + box __________	paint + brush __________
rain + drops __________	finger + nail __________
rail + way __________	rain + bow __________

Letter Teams: ai

When two vowels go walking, the first one does the talking!

The letters **ai** work together to make one sound — the long vowel sound ā, as in *rain (r **ai** n), tail (t **ai** l)* and *wait (w **ai** t)*. It is most often seen in the middle of a word.

SEE & SAY

train	chain	grain	snail
brain	stain	paint	trail
plain	drain	faint	waist

a i

1 Choose words from the *See and Say* list to complete the sentences.

Dad will **p**____________ the fence green.

A **g**____________ of sand is smaller than a **g**____________ of rice.

There is a red beetroot **s**____________ on my white T-shirt.

Pull the plug and let the water **d**____________ away.

2 Write these rhyming words.

aid p______ l______ m______ r______ afr______

3 Complete this table of verbs.

	Add -s	Add -ing	Add -ed
drain			
train			
trail			
stain			

LOOK & LEARN

could would should brown

TARGETING SPELLING 2 © PASCAL PRESS ISBN 9781925490206

4 Name the pictures.

WORD TRAPS

Don't mix up **waist** and **waste**.

*Examples: You wear a belt around your **waist**.*
***Waste** is anything that is not used up, no longer wanted or is left over. If you **waste** something, you are using it up carelessly. Don't **waste** your money. (Don't spend it unwisely.)*

5 Join the syllables to read the words. Match the words to their meanings.

straight en	to make something easy to understand
com plain	to put things in a straight line
ex plain	someone who paints things; an artist
paint er	anything you can put things in
con tain er	to grumble about things

6 Join the compound words to their pictures.

rainbow **chain**saw **waist**coat **drain**pipe **rain**coat

	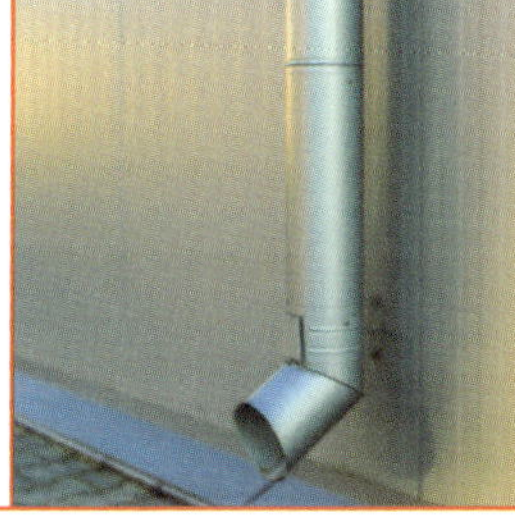			

7 Join the word parts to write these compound words.

hail + storm	______________	nail + brush	______________
sail + boat	______________	brain + wave	______________
rail + road	______________	rain + water	______________

UNIT 19

Letter Teams: ay

The letters **ai** and **ay** have the same sound — the long vowel sound ā. *Examples: rain, tail, day* and *play*
ai is most often seen in the middle of a word.
ay is most often seen at the end of a word.

SEE & SAY

day	may	lay	sway
say	hay	play	stay
way	ray	clay	stray
pay	bay	tray	spray

1 Choose words from the *See and Say* list to complete the sentences.

The ship sailed into the calm waters of the **b**__________.

Today, we will **p**__________ football after school.

Kara and I will **s**__________ on our uncle's farm for a week.

Every **d**__________, we are warmed by the **r**__________**s** of the sun.

Which **w**__________ do I go to get to the river?

2 Complete this table of verbs.

	Add -s	Add -ing	Add -ed
play			
stay			
sway			
spray			

LOOK & LEARN

said
again
away
always

The past tense (time) of say is said (not sayed).

The past tense (time) of pay is paid (not payed).

The past tense (time) of lay is laid (not layed).

TARGETING SPELLING 2 © PASCAL PRESS ISBN 9781925490206

UNIT 19

3 Join the word parts to write these compound words.

play — time ______ / things ______ / ground ______

day — time ______ / light ______ / bed ______

4 Many words begin with the syllable **a** (say *uh*). Mark the words like this: a long. Say all the words aloud.

a long	a gain	a fraid	a bout
a bove	a mong	a lone	a board

5 Join the word parts to write these compound words.

hay + stack haystack

run + way ______

fly + spray ______

take + away ______

day + break ______

hair + spray ______

6 Add a letter team to mend the broken words. Choose between **ai** and **ay**.

We can't pl_ _ outside tod_ _ if it r_ _ns.

"Tra_ _ns run on r_ _l w_ _ lines," s_ _d Dan.

I made a turtle out of cl_ _ and p_ _nted it green.

We saw a ship s_ _ling into the blue waters of the b_ _.

Kay is w_ _ting for the m_ _l to come.

7 Write in the missing words.

There are 24 hours in a d__________.

You must p__________ for the things you buy.

You hit a n__________ with a hammer.

A hen l__________ eggs.

There are many g__________ of sand on a beach.

A fox has a long, bushy t__________.

Football is a game that is p__________ in winter.

You w__________ for a bus at a bus stop.

Letter Teams: ee

The letters **ee** work together to make one sound — the long vowel sound ē. *Examples: sheep (sh* ***ee*** *p), meet (m* ***ee*** *t)*

SEE & SAY

see	queen	week
knee	been	creek
deep	sheet	feed
sheep	meet	need

Write these nouns in plural form. ***(Be careful!)***

knee ______________ sheet ______________ creek ______________

queen ______________ sheep* ______________ foot* ______________

Complete this table of rhyming words.

feed	deep
s	j
w	w
h	p
d	k
r	cr
gr	st

MEMORY TRAINING

Read the words in each list two times. How many words can you remember? Write them in your notebook. Check and write your scores here.

....

LOOK & LEARN

also until four friend

Don't mix up **see** and **sea**.
Examples: You ***see*** *with your eyes. You swim in the* ***sea****.*

Don't mix up **meet** and **meat**.
Examples: To ***meet*** *someone is to come face to face with them.* ***Meat*** *is the flesh of an animal. We often cook and eat* ***meat****.*

Don't mix up **week** and **weak**.
Examples: Seven days make a ***week****. If someone is* ***weak*** *they are not strong.*

TARGETING SPELLING 2 © PASCAL PRESS ISBN 9781925490206

Add an ending to the words in bold. Choose from -s, -ed, -ing, -y and -ly.

UNIT 20

We are **meet**____ our friends in the park.

Cory **feed**____ the hens and **collect**____ the eggs.

The **greed**____ boy ate all the **cake**____ on the plate.

Mum **meet**____ her **friend**____ for coffee **week**____.

The baseball mitt Dad gave me was just what I **need**____.

Write the special past tense (time) verbs.

Present	Past
do	
see	
pay	
feed	

Present	Past
meet	
bleed	
say	
weep	

Join the word parts to make compound words.

bird	skin	week	keeper
wind	end	knee	land
bee	seed	sun	pads
sheep	screen	bee	days
week	hive	Queens	screen

Choose two compound words. Write a sentence about each one.

1 ______________________________

____

2 ______________________________

____

How many words can you remember?

Go back and choose any *See and Say* list. Read through it twice, focusing on how the words look and sound. Write as many words as you can remember in your notebook. Check how many you have written correctly and enter your score here.

Letter Teams: ee

UNIT 21

When two vowels go walking, the first one does the talking!

The letters **ee** work together to make one sound — the long vowel sound ē. *Examples: sheep (sh* ***ee*** *p), meet (m* ***ee*** *t)*

SEE & SAY

tree	sweet	green
free	street	screen
sleep	bleed	freeze
sweep	speed	sneeze

1 Choose words from the *See and Say* list to complete the sentences.

I like **s**____________, juicy grapes.

There are many cars parked in the main **s**____________.

My brother and I **s**____________ in bunk beds.

Mum will **s**____________ the floor with a soft broom.

The car raced around the track at top **s**____________.

2 Complete this table of verbs.

	Present time (add -ing)	Special past time
sleep	sleeping	slept
sweep		
speed		
bleed		
freeze		

3 Write a rhyming word for each of these words.

green	freeze	bleed	sleep	sweet
sh________	squ________	br________	cr________	fl________

LOOK & LEARN

before look new fast

TARGETING SPELLING 2 © PASCAL PRESS ISBN 9781925490206

UNIT 21

4 Add an ending to the words in bold. Choose from -s, -ing, -er, -y and -ly.

A car was seen **speed**_____ through the city **street**_____.

Birds are **sing**_____ **sweet**_____ in the tall **tree**_____.

Mum **keep**_____ ice cream in the **freeze**_____.

Orange_____ are **sweet**_____ than **lemon**_____.

I am **feel**_____ very **sleep**_____, so I will go to bed.

5 Complete this table of rhyming words.

m**eet**	f**eel**
f	h
fl	p
gr	r
sl	kn
tw	wh

MEMORY TRAINING

Read the words in each list two times. How many words can you remember? Write them in your notebook. Check and write your scores here.

....

6 Join the word parts to make compound words.

green	chair	green	barrow
sleep	way	wheel	walk
wheel	house	free	tops
speed	light	sleep	keeper
street	over	tree	way

7 Choose two compound words. Write a sentence about each one.

1 ____

____

2 ____

____

Letter Teams: ea

When two vowels go walking, the first one does the talking!

The letters **ea** work together to make one sound — the long vowel sound ē. *Examples: sea (s **ea**), leaf (l **ea** f), beach (b **ea** ch)*

tea	meal	meat
leaf	real	wheat
beak	seal	beach
weak	heal	teach

e a

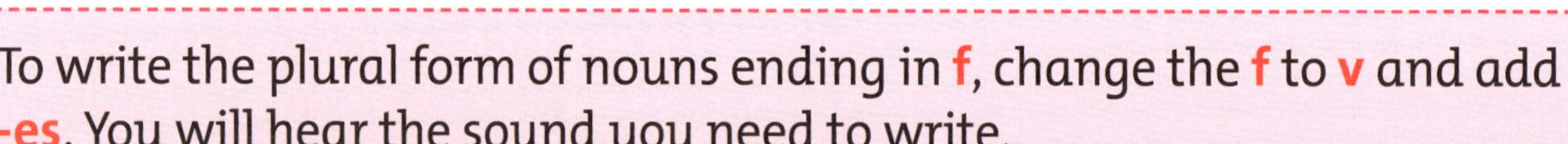

To write the plural form of nouns ending in **f**, change the **f** to **v** and add **-es**. You will hear the sound you need to write.
Examples: leaf, leaves; wolf, wolves; knife, knives. (Exceptions: roofs, chiefs)
If a word ends in **ff**, just add **-s**: *cliff, cliffs*.

1 Write these nouns in plural form.

beak ____________ leaf ____________ meal ____________ beach ____________ teacher ____________

2 Write words that rhyme with eat.

eat				
	b	s	n	h
	ch	bl	tr	pl

3 Name the pictures.

LOOK & LEARN

second next seven eight

TARGETING SPELLING 2 © PASCAL PRESS ISBN 9781925490206

Don't mix up **heal** and **heel**.
*Examples: A doctor **heals** or cures sick people.*
*Your **heel** is the rounded back part of your foot.*
*Shoes have **heels**.*

Don't mix up **real** and **reel**.
Something **real** is something that is true.
*Examples: Her ring is made of **real** gold.*
*You would use a fishing **reel** or a **reel** of cotton.*

4 Add endings to the words in bold to complete the sentences.

teach Miss James is ________________ me how to swim.

leaf Golden ________________ are falling from the trees.

real I am ________________ glad we are going to the zoo.

heal The cut on my arm has ________________ well.

teach Miss Jones is my Year 2 ________________.

5 Join the word parts and write the compound words.

tea
- pot ________________
- cup ________________
- time ________________
- spoon ________________

sea
- shore ________________
- side ________________
- shell ________________
- weed ________________

6 Colour the correct word in the brackets.

I jumped off my [house horse] and hurt my [heal heel].

We had [meat meet] and beans for our [main mane] meal.

Adam took his fishing [reel real] to the [creak creek].

My knees felt [week weak] after a swim in the [see sea].

7 Add letters to mend the broken words. Choose from ee and ea.

Dan has planted b_ _ns, p_ _s and carrot s_ _ds in his garden.

I could s_ _ a gr_ _n bird in the l_ _ves of the gum tr_ _.

We saw a s_ _l sl_ _ping on the rocks at the b_ _ch.

The wind is sw_ _ping the l_ _ves along the str_ _t.

I'm very sl_ _py and I'd r_ _lly like to go to bed.

TARGETING SPELLING 2 © PASCAL PRESS ISBN 9781925490206

Letter Teams: ea

The letters **ea** work together to make one sound — the long vowel sound **ē**. *Examples: steal (st **ea** l), speak (sp **ea** k)*

SEE & SAY

dream	east	bean
cream	feast	clean
scream	least	speak
stream	beast	squeak

1 Choose words from the *See and Say* list to complete the sentences.

I sometimes ________________ of strange beasts when I'm asleep.

The wind is blowing from the ________________.

I ________________ my teeth before I go to bed.

I like peaches and ice ________________.

Our team won the ________________ number of points.

2 Write two rhyming words for each of these words.

each	lead	cream	bean	leak
p	r	t	l	sn
r	b	b	m	cr

LOOK & LEARN

who why which when

3 Ask some questions. Begin with **who**, **why**, **which** or **when**.

____________ do you go to bed?

____________ were you late for school today?

____________ is your best friend?

____________ way do you go to the park?

TARGETING SPELLING 2 © PASCAL PRESS ISBN 9781925490206

Don't mix up **steal** and **steel**.

*Examples: To **steal** is to take something that does not belong to you. **Steel** is a hard, strong building material.*

Don't mix up **creak** and **creek**.
*Examples: If something **creaks**, it makes a squeaking sound. A **creek** is a small stream.*

4 Write words that are opposite in meaning to these words.

dirty ______________ west ______________

most ______________ sour ______________

strong ______________ shallow ______________

5 Add -er to make nouns from these verbs.

teach ______________ freeze ______________

speak ______________ sweep ______________

heal ______________ lead ______________

stream ______________s sneak ______________s

6 Choose a noun from the list above to complete these sentences.

You would wear ______________ on your feet.

A ______________ would work in a school.

You would keep ice cream in a ______________.

You would put ______________ on a Christmas tree.

ICECREAM
750mL

7 Join the word parts to make compound words.

tea	keeper	meal	food
sea	teacher	sea	nuts
shop	time	meat	pod
school	belt	pea	time
seat	bird	seed	ball

8 Choose one compound word and write about it.

____

____

UNIT 24

Letter Teams: le

Many words end in the sound **l**. It is often written as **le**, but the **e** is not sounded. Some words have the same letters in the middle.
*Examples: ke**tt**le, bu**bb**le*
Some have two different letters. *Examples: ha**nd**le, si**mp**le*

SEE & SAY

kettle	paddle	candle	tangle
settle	middle	handle	prickle
wiggle	riddle	rumble	trickle
giggle	cuddle	stumble	simple
saddle	puddle	bangle	pimple

1 **Choose words from the *See and Say* list to complete the sentences.**

I can hear the **r**____________ of thunder.

A cat is sitting in the **m**____________ of the path.

Jill put a **s**____________ and bridle on her horse.

I like to **c**____________ my teddy bear.

John blew out the **c**____________**s** on his birthday cake.

When verbs end in **e**, drop the **e** before adding **-ing**, **-ed** and **-y**.
*Examples: cuddle, cuddl**ing**, cuddl**ed**, cuddl**y***
Just add **-s** to show present time (*cuddle**s***).

2 **Add an ending to the words in bold to complete the sentences.**

wiggle Fran is ________________ her toes in the warm sand.

tangle My fishing line got ________________ in the reeds.

prickle A rose bush is pretty, but it is ________________.

rumble Thunder ________________ and lightning flashed.

trickle Water is ________________ from the garden hose.

LOOK & LEARN happy morning below above

TARGETING SPELLING 2 © PASCAL PRESS ISBN 9781925490206

3 Be a word builder. Double the last letter and add **le**.

*Example: lit, lit**tle***

bat	______	pad	______
rat	______	cat	______
rub	______	bot	______
hob	______	jug	______
net	______	rip	______

4 Complete this table of verbs.

	Add -s	Add -ing	Add -ed
tangle			
wiggle			
trickle			
juggle			

5 Add the missing letter in each word in bold.

Don't **stum__le** and fall into that **pud__le**.

I took an **ap__le** and a **bot__le** of water on my walk.

My knees **trem__le** when I hear the **rum__le** of thunder.

May will **pad__le** her canoe to the **mid__le** of the lake.

I got **tan__led** up in a **pric__ly** bush.

6 Complete this table of verbs.

Add -dle	Add -ble	Add -ple
fon	bub	crum
hud	tum	top
fid	scram	sam

How many words can you remember?

Go back and choose any *See and Say* list. Read through it twice, focusing on how the words look and sound. Write as many words as you can remember in your notebook. Check how many you have written correctly and enter your score here.

1 Name the pictures.

2 Write these nouns in plural form.

peach	______	grain	______	prickle	______
beast	______	creek	______	leaf	______
wheel	______	bean	______	puddle	______
rail	______	handle	______	stream	______

3 Colour the correct word in the brackets.

Our teacher told us the [tail tale] of Peter Rabbit.

I wear sun [scream screen] when I go to the beach.

Zeb will [meet meat] his friends in the park.

There are seven days in a [week weak].

The scratch on my arm will [heel heal] quickly.

4 Write the present tense (time) of these special past time verbs.

Present	Past
sweep	swept
	froze
	laid
	saw

Present	Past
	slept
	paid
	taught
	met

TARGETING SPELLING 2 © PASCAL PRESS ISBN 9781925490206

5 Write words of opposite meaning.

old	______	sad	______	west	______
slow	______	below	______	strong	______
after	______	dirty	______	most	______

6 Add letters to complete the words. Choose from **ee** and **ea**.

The tr_ _s are gr_ _n and the s_ _ is blue.

Last w_ _k, we went fishing in the cr_ _k.

After our main m_ _l, we had p_ _ches and ice cr_ _m.

I'm f_ _ling sl_ _py, so I'll cl_ _n my t_ _th and go to bed.

7 Complete this table of verbs. (*Remember the spelling rules.*)

	Add -s / -es	Add -ing	Add -ed
rain			
sneeze			
stay			
giggle			
clean			

8 Join the word parts to make compound words.

rain	spoon	saddle	shell
tea	house	rain	bars
mail	light	week	coat
beach	bow	sea	bag
street	box	handle	end

9 Circle the spelling mistakes. Write the correct words on the lines.

We saled our boat down the streem. ______ ______

You shud clean your teeth befor bed. ______ ______

Witch way is the mane street? ______ ______

My frend swam to the middel of the lake. ______ ______

UNIT 25

Letter Teams: oa

When two vowels go walking, the first one does the talking!

The letters **oa** work together to make one sound — the long vowel sound ō. *Examples: coat (c **oa** t), croak (cr **oa** k)*

SEE & SAY

boat	goat	goal	road	load
coat	float	foal	toad	loaf

1 Choose words from the *See and Say* list to complete the sentences.

A kid is a baby ________.

A ________ is a baby horse.

Tom will row his ________ across the dam.

The truck is carrying a ________ of bricks.

Jason kicked the first ________ in the soccer match.

2 Write these nouns in plural form.

boat	load	loaf	goal
________	________	________	________
road	goat	toad	coat
________	________	________	________

3 Write a letter in each square to spell the missing words. Here are the clues.

Dan rode his bike down the dusty ____.

A ____ is a frog-like creature.

Our team scored four ____ in the football game.

Mum will buy two ____ of bread and some buns.

On cold days, I wear a ____ to school.

r					
t					
g					
l					
c					

LOOK & LEARN

Sunday love along only

TARGETING SPELLING 2 © PASCAL PRESS ISBN 9781925490206

Add **oa** to complete these words. Say the words aloud.

l____n r____m c____l

gr____n f____m sh____l

Don't mix up lone and loan.

Lone is having no one with you.
Example: A ***lone*** *fox approached the henhouse.*

A **loan** is something that is borrowed and returned.
Examples: I gave Thomas a ***loan*** *of my pencil.*
Can you ***loan*** *me your ruler?*

Add endings to the words in bold to complete the sentences.

load The men ________________ coal into railway trucks.

loaf I got two ________________ of bread at the baker's shop.

float Clouds are ________________ across the sky.

coat Dad put three ________________ of paint on my billycart.

Join the word parts to make compound words.

rain	shed	over	keeper
boat	coat	goat	works
road	stool	goal	herd
toad	way	road	coat

Choose three compound words and write about them.

1 ____

____

2 ____

____

3 ____

____

Letter Teams: oa

When two vowels go walking, the first one does the talking!

The letters **oa** work together to make one sound — the long vowel sound ō. *Examples: coat (c **oa** t), croak (cr **oa** k)*

toast	coach	moan	soak	soap
coast	poach	groan	croak	throat

1 Write these nouns in plural form.

coast	coach	toaster	throat
___________	___________	___________	___________

2 Add endings to the words in bold to complete the sentences.

Mr Timms **coach**_____ our team on **Monday**_____.

I **poach**_____ the eggs and Rosie **toast**_____ the bread.

We could hear frogs **croak**_____ and goats **bleat**_____.

Before I ate lunch, I **wash**_____ my **hand**_____ in hot, **soap**_____ water.

3 Colour the pairs of words that have *almost* the same meaning. Use a different colour for each pair.

coach	road	boat	coat	coast	moan
ship	shore	bus	groan	highway	jacket

4 Write in the missing words.

Our football **c**_____________ gave us a pep talk before the game.

We sailed along the **c**_____________ in our sailing **b**_____________.

I had **p**_____________ed eggs and **t**_____________ for breakfast.

Jess has a cold and a sore **th**_____________.

LOOK & LEARN

Monday work won because

TARGETING SPELLING 2 © PASCAL PRESS ISBN 9781925490206

5 Draw a line to match the compound words and pictures.

rollercoaster **toad**stool **coast**line **goal**post **cock**roach

6 Colour the correct word in the brackets.

Holly scored the first [goal gold] of the game.

The sunflower has [groan grown] very quickly.

The men loaded the [cold coal] into the ship's hold.

Ben gave me a [lone loan] of his baseball mitt.

Dad [towed toad] a caravan behind his 4WD.

7 Look for these oa words in the word search.

coaches
soapy
roast
moan
croaky
toaster
coat
toad

c	e	n	c	o	a	t
r	i	s	o	a	p	y
o	n	c	a	r	p	t
a	a	f	c	d	w	s
k	o	g	h	a	l	a
y	m	t	e	o	b	o
t	o	a	s	t	e	r

8 Unscramble these four-letter words. All words have oa in them.

amno	olfa	caot	psao	dola
______	______	______	______	______
loag	tabo	akos	atog	nlao
______	______	______	______	______

UNIT 27

Letter Teams: ow

Like **oa**, the letters **ow** work together to make one sound — the long vowel sound ō. *Examples: snow (sn* ***ow****), grow (gr* ***ow****)*
Note that **oa** is the middle sound in a word, and **ow** is an end sound.

SEE & SAY

snow	flow	arrow	yellow
slow	show	barrow	bellow
blow	mow	burrow	follow
grow	low	borrow	hollow
know	row	tomorrow	shallow

1 Add endings to the words in bold to complete the sentences.

I went to the zoo the **follow**______ day.

A cold wind is **blow**______ across the **snow**______ fields.

A wombat is a large **burrow**______ animal.

The children are **throw**______ **snowball**______ at each other.

Men once hunted with **bow**______ and **arrow**______.

2 Write these *snow* words.

snow
- ball ____________
- man ____________
- storm ____________
- flakes ____________

3 Colour the pairs of words that are opposite in meaning. Use a different colour for each pair.

deep	fast	below	sweet	sink	high
above	float	sour	low	slow	shallow

LOOK & LEARN

Tuesday move almost because

TARGETING SPELLING 2 © PASCAL PRESS ISBN 9781925490206

Write the words from the word wheel.

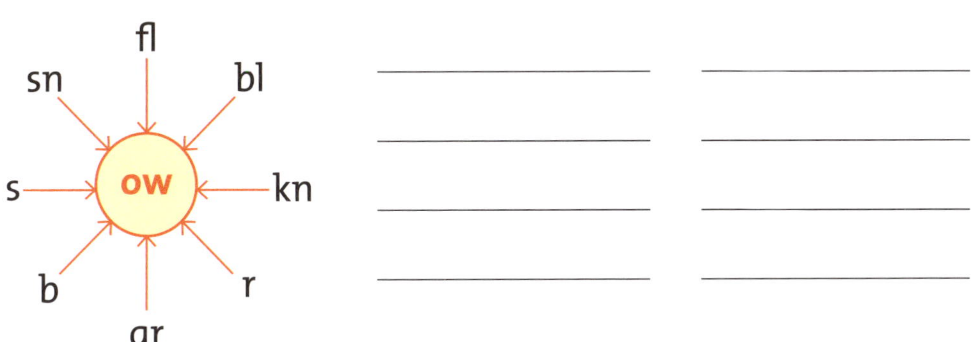

______	______
______	______
______	______
______	______

Don't mix up **sow** and **sew**.
*Examples: You **sow** seeds, but you **sew** with a needle and cotton.*

Join the word parts to make compound words.

show + time	showtime	side + show	______
row + boat	______	rain + bow	______
show + room	______	lawn + mower	______
blow + hole	______	wheel + barrow	______

Some verbs have a special past time form when they follow **has**, **have** and **had**.
*Examples: I show, I showed, I **have shown**;*
*He throws, He threw, He **has thrown**.*

Using the tip above, complete this table of verbs.

Present time	Past time	
They show	They showed	They have shown
It flies	It flew	It had
He sows	He sowed	He has
They grow	They grew	They have
She knows	She knew	She has
It blows	It blew	It had

UNIT 28

Letter Teams: ar

The letter team **ar** is the **ah** sound in *car* and *star*. Sometimes, the letter **a** has the same **ah** sound. *Examples: class, grass, pass*

SEE & SAY

car	far	park	spark
bar	farm	dark	bark
jar	arm	shark	mark

Write these nouns in plural form.

car ______ arm ______ spark ______ jar ______ park ______

Write the words that rhyme with art.

art	
p	c
d	st
sm	ch

MEMORY TRAINING

Read the words in the list two times. How many words can you remember? Write them in your notebook. Check and write your score here.

....

Mend the broken words. All words have ar in them.

The dog **b**_ _**k**_ _ at every **c**_ _ that drove by.

A **sh**_ _ _ is a very large fish with very **sh**_ _ _ teeth.

The **f**_ _**m**_ _ takes the eggs to **m**_ _**k**_ _.

Don't walk in the **p**_ _ _ after **d**_ _ _.

Name the pictures.

TARGETING SPELLING 2 © PASCAL PRESS ISBN 9781925490206

Wednesday beside between among

5 Add be- and a- to complete the words.

Add be-		Add a-	
____fore	____side	__way	__mong
____low	____neath	__long	__gain
____cause	____long	__bove	__bout
____gin	____come	__sleep	__wake
____gan	____came	__part	__round

When a word ends in **ar**, add **-r** before adding **-ing**, **-ed** or **-y**.
Examples: star, starring, starry

6 Add endings to the words in bold to complete the sentences.

park Dad ____________________ the car in the main street.

sparkle The lake is ____________________ in the sunshine.

jar Jim jumped off his billycart and ____________________ his arm.

mark The teacher hasn't ____________________ my homework.

bar A brick wall rose before us, ____________________ our way.

7 Be a word builder. Join the syllables and write the words.

spark + le	sparkle	farm + er	____________
bar + ber	____________	mark + et	____________
arm + y	____________	dark + en	____________
re + mark	____________	car + pen + ter	____________
doll + ar	____________	coll + ar	____________

How many words can you remember?

Go back and choose any *See and Say* list. Read through it twice, focusing on how the words look and sound. Write as many words as you can remember in your notebook. Check how many you have written correctly and enter your score here.

UNIT 29

Letter Teams: ar

The letter team **ar** is the **ah** sound in *car* and *star*. Sometimes, the letter **a** has the same **ah** sound. *Examples: class, grass, pass*

SEE & SAY

yard	guard	arch	star
card	art	march	start
hard	smart	scarf	sharp

Write these nouns in plural form. * *Remember the f rule.*

star	march	yard	guard	scarf*
____	____	____	____	____

Add ar to complete these words. Say the words aloud two times then write as many as you can remember in your notebook.

ch____t	h____sh	sn____l
h____p	ch____m	c____ve

Join the word parts and write the compound words.

farm — house ____, land ____, work ____, yard ____

car — port ____, sick ____, pet ____, go ____

Write these two-syllable words.

arch + er	archer	mar + ble	____
art + ist	____	star + tle	____
part + ner	____	part + y	____
tar + get	____	sharp +en	____

LOOK & LEARN

Thursday eye blue unless

5 Complete this table of verbs.

	Add -s / -es	Add -ing	Add -ed
startle			
march			
guard			
carve			

When a word ends in **ar**, add **-r** before adding **-ing**, **-ed** or **-y**.
Examples: bar, barring, barred

6 Add endings to complete the words in bold.

The soldiers are **march**_____ down the street in straight **line**_____.

The boys **start**_____ to play a game of **marble**_____.

We **look**_____ up into the **star**_____ night sky.

An **arch**_____ would use **bow**_____ and **arrow**_____.

The farmer's dog is **guard**_____ the **duck**_____ and **hen**_____.

7 Write in the names of five colours.

8 Write in the names of five days of the week.

9 Join the word parts to make compound words.

life →	phone	park	yard
over	guard	art	board
smart	scarf	barn	way
arm	board	dart	work
head	pit	arch	land

Letter Teams: or, ore

The letter team **or** is usually found in the middle of words. Add an **-e** if the **or** sound is on the end. *Examples: storm, short; store, score*
This sound is also written as **aw** *(saw)*, **au** *(caught)* and **our** *(court)*.

SEE & SAY

form	worn	bore	core
storm	torn	more	store
horse	torch	wore	shore
horn	sport	sore	snore
born	short	tore	score

Write these nouns in plural form.

horse	torch	store	sport	horn
___________	___________	___________	___________	___________

Write the rhyming words.

ford	c	l	sw
fort	p	s	sn

Colour the pairs of words that make a compound word. Use a different colour for each pair.

score	store	sports	thunder	sea	torch
ground	light	board	shore	storm	room

LOOK & LEARN

Friday often pretty shoe

WORD TRAPS

Don't mix up **four** and **for**.
Four is a number (4). **For** is a word that begins a phrase.
*Examples: **for** you; **for** me; **for** five days; **for** a bus ride; **for** Joe*

TARGETING SPELLING 2 © PASCAL PRESS ISBN 9781925490206

Complete this table of verbs.

UNIT 30

	Add -s	Add -ing	Add -ed
storm			
score			
store			
snore			

Some verbs have a special past time form when they follow **has**, **have** and **had**.
*Examples: I wear, I wore, I **have worn**; He tears, He tore, He **has torn***

5 Add the correct word. Choose from more and most.

I have saved __________ money than my sister.

__________ of the children in my class own pets.

Jen got the __________ words right in the spelling test.

Do you want some __________ to eat?

This game needs __________ than six players.

6 Mend the broken words. All have or in them.

Throw your apple **c**_ _ _ in the bin.

I rode my **h**_ _ _ _ along the sandy **sh**_ _ _.

The cow had **sh**_ _ _, sharp **h**_ _ _ _.

On **sp**_ _ _ _ day, I **w**_ _ _ a yellow T-shirt and black **sh**_ _ _ _.

I bought a battery for my **t**_ _ _ _ at the **st**_ _ _.

7 Write about your favourite sport.

____

____

____

____

____

____

UNIT 31

Syllables

Syllables are the chunks of sounds you can hear in a word. **Dog** has 🖐 syllable, **kit ten** has 🖐🖐, **lem on ade** has 🖐🖐🖐 and **hel i cop ter** has 🖐🖐🖐🖐. How many **syllables** are in your first name?

SEE & SAY

kitten	toffee	jacket	pumpkin
button	coffee	packet	custard
puppet	carrot	pocket	mustard
kennel	parrot	rocket	trumpet
funnel	possum	napkin	crumpet

Name the pictures.

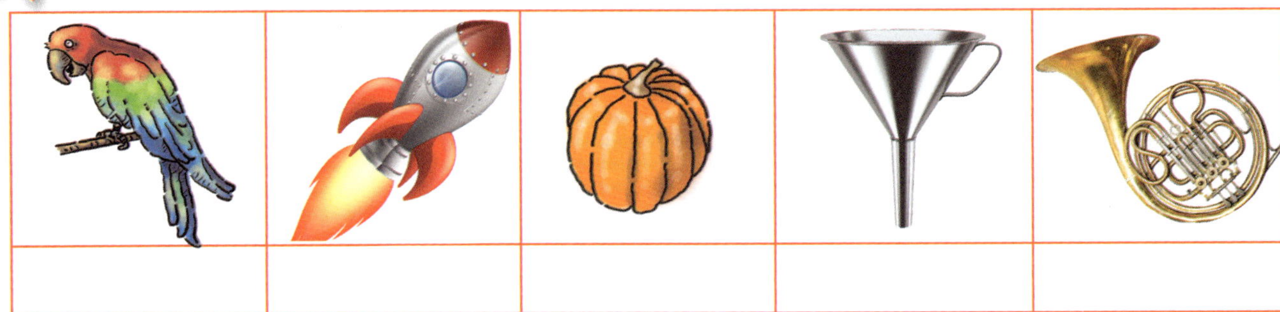

Write these nouns in plural form.

puppet ____________ button ____________ napkin ____________ jacket ____________ kitten ____________

Join the syllables to write the words. Read them to a classmate.

ham | mer	hammer	man | go	____________
stop | per	____________	win | dow	____________
but | ter	____________	han | dle	____________
pep | per	____________	num | ber	____________
ap | ple	____________	lob | ster	____________

LOOK & LEARN Saturday begin behind house

TARGETING SPELLING 2 © PASCAL PRESS ISBN 9781925490206

Here are some pop/u/lar sports. Match them to their pictures.

bad/min/ton crick/et arch/er/y soc/cer hock/ey

5 What am I? Here are the clues.

a house for a dog	k__________
a baby cat	k__________
a doll worked by strings	p__________
an Australian night-hunting animal	p__________
worn on cold days	j__________
a root vegetable, orange in colour	c__________
a hot drink made from brown beans	c__________
a bird with brightly coloured feathers	p__________
played in a band	t__________
the day after Friday	S__________

6 Here are some supermarket words. Clap the syllables. Write a syllable in each box.

crackers		
chicken		
biscuits		
yoghurt		
honey		

lemonade			
spaghetti			
Vegemite			
chocolate			
potatoes			

UNIT 32 Homophones

Homophones are words that sound the same, but have a different spelling. *Examples: no/know; not/knot; tail/tale; ate/eight; for/four; main/mane; where/wear*

SEE & SAY

mail	male	see	sea	rode	road	sore	saw
pail	pale	reel	real	ate	eight	wore	war
sail	sale	week	weak	by	buy	for	four
pain	pane	meet	meat	no	know	to, too, two	
plain	plane	be	bee	here	hear	new	knew

1 Choose a word from the *See and Say* list to complete the sentences.

I went to a sports shop to **b**__________ a cricket bat and ball.

There are seven days in a **w**__________.

Did you **h**__________ someone calling my name?

We **s**__________ tigers and elephants at the zoo.

2 Colour the word that matches each picture.

	4			8	2
plane	for	pail	meat	eight	to / two
plain	four	pale	meet	ate	too

3 Write a homophone *(same sound, different spelling)* for each word.

bean	__________	wail	__________
creak	__________	maid	__________
heal	__________	waist	__________
steal	__________	pain	__________

LOOK & LEARN

until past front able

TARGETING SPELLING 2 © PASCAL PRESS ISBN 9781925490206

Complete this table of rhyming words.

past	able
f	t
m	c
l	f
c	st

MEMORY TRAINING

UNIT 32

Read the words in the list two times. How many words can you remember? Write them in your notebook. Check and write your scores here.

....

Colour the correct word in the brackets.

Billy has a model [plain plane] and I'd like one [to too].

After her illness, Lara was [pail pale] and [weak week].

Alfie will [be bee] [ate eight] years old tomorrow.

Jenny [road rode] her motor scooter down to the [see sea].

How do you get a baby astronaut to sleep? To find out, colour the letter before the correct answer to spell it out.

Simon has a new fishing rod and ____.	r	reel	s	real
Kara ____ a gold chain around her neck.	i	war	o	wore
Do you ____ how to make a paper plane?	n	no	c	know
I bought a pair of jeans at the ____.	k	sale	g	sail
Can you ____ the foxes barking?	l	here	i	hear
My birthday gift came in the ____.	t	mail	y	male

You _ _ _ _ - _ _.

How many words can you remember?

Go back and choose any *See and Say* list. Read through it twice, focusing on how the words look and sound. Write as many words as you can remember in your notebook. Check how many you have written correctly and enter your score here.

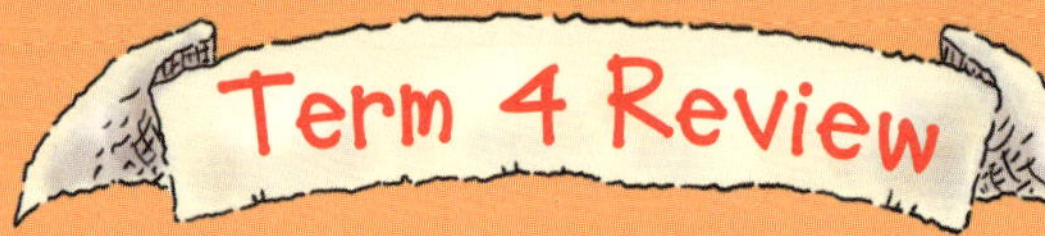

1 Name the pictures.

2 Write these nouns in plural form.

goat	______	coach	______	loaf	______
guard	______	scarf	______	arm	______
torch	______	score	______	show	______
week	______	plane	______	arch	______

3 Write words of opposite meaning.

fast	______	finish	______	long	______
soft	______	high	______	near	______
light	______	strong	______	sink	______

4 Colour the correct word in the brackets.

A [fold foal] is a baby [horse house].

This is a [tale tail] about a pesky [towed toad].

We could [here hear] a truck coming along the [rode road].

Tim has [grown groan] tall since I last [sore saw] him.

TARGETING SPELLING 2 © PASCAL PRESS ISBN 9781925490206

Term 4 Review

5 Write in the missing words.

Fraser is sitting **be**__________ his friend Thomas.

I feed my pet rabbit each day **be**__________ I go to school.

We can't play tennis **be**________________ it is raining.

Zac hid **be**__________ a tree and I couldn't see him.

Our swimming lesson will **be**__________ at ten o'clock.

6 Complete this table of verbs.

	Add -s / -es	Add -ing	Add -ed
snow			
march			
sparkle			
bar			

7 Monday is the first day of the week. Name the other days.

_______________ _______________ _______________

_______________ _______________ _______________

8 Complete this table of special past time verbs.

I wear	I wore	I have worn
Paper tears	It	It has
Flowers grow	They	They have
Wind blows	It	It has

9 Join the word parts to make compound words.

life	bow	boat	horse
roller	works	goal	coat
rain	jacket	stage	shed
road	scarf	rain	posts
head	coaster	race	coach

The Top 3 Spelling Rules

Rules	How to apply the rule	Examples
1 Doubling rule	When there is only ONE consonant after a short vowel, **double** that consonant before you add *-ing*, *-ed*, *-y*, *-er* or *-est*.	hop hopping skip skipped fun funny big bigger biggest
	If there are already TWO consonants after the short vowel, just add an ending.	jump jumping pack packed dust dusty rich richer richest
2 The *e* rule	When a word ends in *e*, drop the *e* before you add an ending that begins with a vowel or *y*.	ride riding shine shiny prickle prickly
	Do NOT drop the *e* when adding *-ly* (or any suffix beginning with a consonant).	safe safely safety use useful useless
3 The *y* rule	When a noun ends in *y*, follow these simple rules to write its plural: 1 If the letter before the *y* is a vowel, just add *-s*. 2 If the letter before the *y* is NOT a vowel, change *y* to *i* and add *-es*.	boys days monkeys baby babies lady ladies
	When a regular verb ends in *y*, follow these simple rules to write it in present or past tense: 1 Just add *-ing*. 2 If the letter before the *y* is a vowel, just add *-s* or *-ed*. 3 If the letter before the *y* is NOT a vowel, change *y* to *i* and add *-es* or *-ed*.	fly flying carry carrying play plays played enjoy enjoys enjoyed cry cries cried hurry hurries hurried
	When an adjective ends in *y*, change *y* to *i* and add *-er* or *-est* (comparing) and *-ly* (adverbs of manner).	happier happiest happily lazier laziest lazily

Common Endings

Ending	Purpose	Examples	Rule
-s	Add *-s* to MOST nouns to write them in plural form.	dogs apples toys hats	
	Add *-s* to present tense verbs when the subject is *'he'*, *'she'* or *'it'*.	runs plays rains growls eats stares swims	
-es	Add *-es* to nouns and verbs that end in *s*, *ss*, *z*, *zz*, *x*, *sh*, *ch*.	buses dishes foxes tosses buzzes itches	
-ing	Add *-ing* to verbs to make present participles.	going jumping crying hopping riding	1, 2, 3
-ed	Add *-ed* to *regular* verbs to make past participles.	planted clapped played carried baked	1, 2, 3
-y	Add *-y* to form adjectives.	bumpy funny stony	1, 2
-er -est	Add *-er* or *-est* to show how adjectives and adverbs compare.	taller tallest bigger biggest busier busiest nicer nicest	1, 2, 3
-ly	Add *-ly* to form adverbs of manner.	quickly lately noisily	2, 3

TARGETING SPELLING 2 © PASCAL PRESS ISBN 9781925490206